THE WORD IN WORSHIP

Dramatic Scripture Arrangements for Performance and Liturgy

by
Paul M. Miller and Jeff Wyatt

Printed in the United States of America

Permission to reproduce these Scripture arangements and interpolations for worship services use is granted with the inclusion of the permission line that appears with each selection.

Some minor adaptations have been made in the wording of certain NIV passages, simply to insure clear communication within the script format.

Cover art by Paul Franitza

Contents

A Rationale for Reading Scripture in Worship 6

The Word in Worship: Rehearsing the Faith

■ **Old Testament Narratives**

God Will Provide 11
The Anointing of David 12
Shadrach, Meshach, Abednego, and the Fiery Furnace 13
The Faithful 16

■ **Gospel Narratives**

God with Us 19
To Us a Son Is Given 20
Gifts for a King 22
Christ's Mission 24
The Prophet in His Hometown 24
The Man Born Blind 25
Life Comes to Dry Bones 28
In Remembrance of Me 30
Who Is My Accuser? 32
The King of the Jews 33
It Is Finished 34
We Have Seen the Lord 36
The Emmaus Road Incident 37

■ **Early Christian Narratives**

The Day of Pentecost 39
Stephen 40
Philip and the Ethiopian 43

The Word in Worship: Reaffirming the Faith

■ **This We Believe**

The Mercy of God 47
All We like Sheep 49
All Have Sinned 51
The Kingship of Christ 52
The Word Made Flesh 53

God's Ordinances ... 55
Salvation ... 55
The New Birth ... 57
Security in Christ ... 58
The Beatitudes ... 58
The Message of the Cross ... 59
Light ... 60
A Light for the Gentiles ... 61

■ They'll Know That We Are Christians . . .

A Litany of Beginning ... 63
Responding to God's Word ... 64
True Fasting ... 65
Obedience and Disobedience ... 66
Love, Not Sacrifice ... 67
Social Justice ... 68
Positive Christian Living ... 69
Assurance ... 71
Christian Conduct ... 71
While It Is Yet Day ... 72
The Day Is Almost Here ... 73
Come, Lord Jesus! ... 74

■ The Family of God

What God Has Joined ... 75
A Wedding Ceremony Reading ... 76
For Christian Parents ... 77
Members Together of One Body ... 77

The Word in Worship: Reflecting the Faith

■ Celebrating His Goodness

The Earth Is the Lord's ... 81
The Good Things of God ... 82
Gratitude ... 83
He Who Comes in the Name of the Lord ... 84
Joy in the Lord ... 85
Marks of a Christian ... 86
To Heal the Suffering ... 87
Glory Forever! ... 88
What God Has Prepared ... 88

■ Claiming the Promises

The Song of Moses ... 89
God's Provisions ... 90
God's Justice ... 91
His Promises ... 92

Together with Him 92
The New Jerusalem 93

■ **Waiting and Trusting**
David's God: King and Shepherd 95
The Lord Is My Shepherd 96
Waiting and Trusting 97
In the Potter's Hand 98
To All Who Thirst 99
In Christ 100

Scripture Index 101
Seasonal and Topical Index 104

A Rationale for Reading Scripture in Worship

QUESTION: So why is it important for a congregation to read Scripture aloud in public worship?

ANSWER: First of all, there is a wonderful tradition that transcends any organized church; it's a practice that has history on its side—the oral sharing of the Word of God.

Long before the Scriptures were turned out on the Gutenberg press or illuminated by cloistered monks, the first five books of Moses, the Prophets, Psalms and Proverbs, Jesus' parables, Paul's and John's Epistles, as well as the Apocalypse of John, were proclaimed orally. They were declared to congregations through the medium of the human voice and spirit.

"But we've tried it, and it's so uninspiring—those long and difficult-to-read responsive readings in the back of the hymnal."

"And there are all those words that only a seminarian can pronounce. I don't want to be embarrassed when I have to read the word *concupiscence.*"

All right, let's talk about it.

* * *

Picture the small sanctuary of St. James by Wal-Mart. The occasion is Sunday worship during Advent. Three candles flicker in the boughs of a natural evergreen wreath—no plastic here. Their flames reflect on the brass vases of scarlet poinsettias on either side. High above the Communion tables glows a stained-glass window depicting an open Bible with the legend, "Thy Word Is Light."

From the lectern side of the chancel the worship leader announces the readings for the third Sunday of Advent. All hands turn to the day's liturgy. Age-old words are read together by the congregation; some of it is Scripture, while other expressions are inspired prose written by men and women of conviction by which the worshiper regularly affirms his and her faith and intentions.

Participation has been the aim of the liturgical worship service through the ages. Historical evidence seems to indicate that first-century believers recited and read together when they gathered on the Lord's Day.

Today, most evangelical believers feel that while the repeated scriptures and scriptural allusions are often meaningful and may strike a responsive chord, their form and sometimes antique language invalidates the worship experience for the born again.

To the person raised in the liturgical tradition, the words and forms can be overly familiar, with a resulting spirit of "I've heard it all before." To these worshipers, the beauty and message of the readings have been lost through uninvolved use and the words' seeming disregard of contemporary life. Nonetheless, every Sunday morning, communicants in liturgical services throughout the world continue to read the words of life that have the potential to change lives.

In contrast, a rapidly growing segment of evangelical churches are parting from their tried and true worship forms in an attempt to generate greater interest and involvement in the Word. More often than not, their goal is to reach the generations that have been influenced by the pacing and techniques of MTV and "Sesame Street." The resulting commonality appears to be a performance form of worship, with skilled and highly rehearsed leadership in front of a congregation that responds with its emotions and senses, not just its intellect. There is an excitement and enthusiasm about this style of service that makes it contemporary and emotionally satisfying.

In such a setting, Scripture is more often sung as choruses than read aloud by the congregation. The corporate reading of Scripture in this new tradition has been considered by some to be a hindrance to a relevant service format. One correspondent, in reflecting on the traditional use of the back-of-the-hymnal responsive reading, wrote that reading aloud in a service can be an embarrassment to the uninitiated to whom the service is directed. "We feel that most of the unchurched are not used to reading aloud. The sound of their own voice and inability to sight-read are problematic."

While the influence of the so-called seekers service, in which everything is designed to appeal to the unchurched, has been pioneered by churches in the Reformed tradition and independent community churches, the sweeping charismatic revival with its resulting influence has also affected our patterns of worship, often contributing to a worship format that encourages self-expression, including dancing in the Spirit and the sharing of an individual's words of truth and prophecy, which is often the time in a service for sharing God's Word by the congregation.

While the expressions and forms are divergent, there is actually a common denominator between liturgical and what is called contemporary free church worship—that is the recognition that the Bible is central to all we teach, and it must be incorporated into worship. The contention seems to be how the Word is expressed in worship.

This brings us to our purpose in writing this book. Both of us are convinced that the rigidly structured liturgical service usually needs an infusion of relevance and the contemporary in its forms. On the other hand, we are aware that Scripture and paraphrases set as catchy choruses may not necessarily promote participation. All of us have been in services where the uninitiated, including us, are not familiar with the chorus tunes and figurative scriptural language and have not been touched by the worship experience that others were enjoying. Some are not aware that the words being sung are from the Bible.

That is the point of this collection. It is our goal to present God's Word in dramatic, easy-to-read arrangements and interpolations that encourage relevant participation by the congregation, the worship leader, choir members, and specially designated solo readers. Because there is a place in creative worship planning for Scripture songs, even as there is for liturgy that speaks to the heart, we are not suggesting that musical expressions be limited; we are underscoring that the worshiper ought to be given an opportunity to speak the Word of God, and in doing so, to connect with the rich oral tradition that speaks to the heart and to the mind.

A Personal Word

The preparation of this scriptural material has been a labor of love for both of us. Over and over again, while working at our separate word processors, we have reexperienced the power of God's written Word. In our own ministries we have discovered that except for the Holy Spirit, nothing can enhance the meaning and personal response to Scripture like the human voice. While music will often provide a glorious and emotional response, a thoughtfully proclaimed passage of the Word can certainly fulfill the description:

> The word of God is living and active. Sharper than any double-edged sword, it penetrates even to dividing soul and spirit, joints and marrow; it judges the thoughts and attitudes of the heart.
>
> Hebrews 4:12

To this we say, "Amen."

Paul M. Miller and Jeff Wyatt
Kansas City

The Word in Worship:

Rehearsing the Faith

God Will Provide

Narrator 1: There was a time when God tested Abraham. He said to him,

Solo 1: Abraham!

Solo 2: Here I am, God.

Solo 1: Abraham, take your son, your only son, Isaac, whom you love, and go to the region of Moriah.

Solo 2: And . . .

Solo 1: And sacrifice Isaac there as a burnt offering.

Narr. 2: Early the next morning Abraham got up and saddled his donkey.

Narr. 1: He took with him two of his servants . . .

Narrs. 1 & 2: And his son Isaac.

Narr. 2: When he had cut enough wood for the burnt offering, he set out for the place God had told him about.

Narr. 1: On the third day Abraham looked up and saw the place of sacrifice in the distance.

Solo 2: You servants, stay here with the donkey while I and the boy go over there. We will worship and then we will come back to you.

Narr. 2: Abraham took the wood for the burnt offering and placed it on his son Isaac, and he himself carried the fire and the knife.

Narr. 1: As the two of them went on together, Isaac spoke up,

Solo 1: Father?

Solo 2: Yes, my son?

Solo 1: The fire and the wood are here, but where is the lamb?

Narr. 1: The father paused for just a minute, then spoke in confidence,

Solo 2: My son, God himself will provide the lamb for the burnt offering.

Narr. 1: Then the two of them went on together.

Narr. 2: When they reached the place God had told him about, Abraham built an altar and arranged the wood on it. He bound his son Isaac and laid him on the altar.

Narr. 1: Then he reached out his hand and took the knife and raised his arm to sacrifice his son.

Solo 1: Abraham! Stop! Do not lay a hand on the boy. Do not do anything to him.

Narr. 2: A voice from heaven stopped the old man.

Solo 1: Now I know that you fear God, because you have not withheld from me your son, your only son.

NARR. 1: Abraham looked up and there in a thicket he saw a ram caught by its horns.

NARR. 2: He took the ram and sacrificed it as a burnt offering instead of his son.

SOLO 2: I will call this place "The Lord Will Provide."

NARR. 2: And the angel of the Lord said,

SOLO 1: Because you have done this and have not withheld your son, your only son, I will bless you . . . and through your offspring all nations on earth will be blessed, because you have obeyed me.

NARR. 1: Then Abraham and Isaac set off together for home.

SOLO 2: See, son? I said God would provide!

GENESIS 22:1-19

The Anointing of David

LEADER: Saul the king had been rejected by the Lord, and Samuel the prophet went to Jesse to make sacrifice and to anoint a new king from among Jesse's sons.

SAMUEL: I am Samuel and I have come in peace, Jesse. I have come to consecrate you and your boys, Eliab, Abinadab, Shammah, Nethanel, Raddai, Ozem—

JESSE *(interrupting):* Here, Samuel, this is my son Eliab.

SAMUEL: Ah, Lord, this Eliab must be your anointed—the next king of Israel.

LEADER: But the Lord said to Samuel, "Do not consider his appearance or his height, for I have rejected him. The Lord does not look at the things man looks at."

SAMUEL: I know, Lord, man looks at the outward appearance, but you, Lord, look at the heart.

JESSE: Then I will call my next son, Abinadab.

SAMUEL: No, Jesse, the Lord has not chosen this one either.

LEADER: Jesse then had Shammah pass by, but Samuel said,

SAMUEL: Nor has the Lord chosen this one.

LEADER: So Jesse had seven of his sons pass before Samuel, but Samuel said to him,

SAMUEL: The Lord has not chosen these. Are these all the sons you have?

JESSE: There is still the youngest, but he is tending the sheep.

SAMUEL: Well, send for him, Jesse; we will not sit down until he arrives.

LEADER: So Jesse sent for David and had the boy brought in.

Samuel: He is a ruddy and handsome boy, Jesse.

Leader: The the Lord said, "Rise and anoint the boy David; he is the one who shall be king of Israel."

Samuel: Yes, Lord.

Leader: So Samuel took the horn of oil and anointed David in the presence of his brothers.

Samuel: And from this day on, David, the Spirit of the Lord will be upon you in power.

Leader: Perhaps this is what David remembered in later years when he wrote:

David:
The Lord is my light and my salvation—
whom shall I fear?
The Lord is the stronghold of my life—
of whom shall I be afraid?
I am still confident of this:
I will see the goodness of the Lord
in the land of the living.
Wait for the Lord;
be strong and take heart
and wait for the Lord.

1 Samuel 16:1-13; Psalm 27:1, 13-14

Shadrach, Meshach, Abednego, and the Fiery Furnace

Narr. 1: King Nebuchadnezzar made an image of gold, ninety feet high and nine feet wide, and set it up on the plain of Dura in the province of Babylon.

Narr. 2: He then summoned the satraps, prefects, governors, advisers, treasurers, judges, magistrates and all the other provincial officials to come to the dedication of the image that King Nebuchadnezzar had set up, and they stood before it.

Narr. 3: Then the herald boldly proclaimed:

Herald: This is what you are commanded to do, O peoples, nations and men of every language: As soon as you hear the sound of the horn *[optional music*]*, flute *[music]*, zither *[music]*, lyre *[music]*, harp *[music]*, pipes *[music]* and all kinds of music, you must fall down and worship the image of gold that King Nebuchadnezzar has set up. Whoever does not fall down and worship will immediately be thrown into a blazing furnace.

Narr. 1: Therefore, as soon as they heard the sound of the horn *[music]*, flute *[music]*, zither *[music]*, lyre *[music]*, harp *[music]*, pipes *[music]* and all kinds of music, all the peoples, nations and men of every language fell down and worshiped the image that King Nebuchadnezzar had set up.

*Optional piano chord or bells ring to underscore musical idea.

Narr. 2: At this time some astrologers came forward and denounced the Jews.

Narr. 3: They said to King Nebuchadnezzar,

Astrologer 1: O king, live forever!

Astrologer 2: You have issued a decree, O king, that everyone who hears the sound of the horn *[music]*, flute *[music]*, . . .

Astrologer 1: Zither *[music]*, lyre *[music]*, harp *[music]*, pipes *[music]* . . .

Astrologer 2: And all kinds of music must fall down and worship the image of gold.

Astrologer 1: And that whoever does not fall down and worship will be thrown into a blazing furnace.

Astrologer 2: But there are some Jews whom you have set over the affairs of the province of Babylon—

Astrologer 1: Shadrach, Meshach and Abednego—

Astrologer 2: Who pay no attention to you, O king.

Astrologer 1: They neither serve your gods nor worship the image of gold you have set up.

Narr. 1: With furious rage, Nebuchadnezzar summoned Shadrach, Meshach and Abednego.

Narr. 2: So these men were brought before the king,

Narr. 3: And Nebuchadnezzar said to them,

Nebuchadnezzar: Is it true, Shadrach, Meshach and Abednego, that you do not serve my gods or worship the image of gold that I have set up? Now when you hear the sound of the horn *[music]*, flute *[music]*, zither *[music]*, lyre *[music]*, harp *[music]*, pipes *[music]* and all kinds of music, if you are ready to fall down and worship the image I made, very good. But if you do not worship it, you will be thrown immediately into a blazing furnace. Then what god will be able to rescue you from my hand?

Narr. 3: Shadrach, Meshach and Abednego replied to the king.

Shadrach: O Nebuchadnezzar, we need not defend ourselves before you in this matter.

Meshach: If we are thrown into the blazing furnace, the God we serve is able to save us from it, and he will rescue us from your hand, O king.

Abednego: But even if he does not, we want you to know, O king, we will not serve your gods or worship the image of gold you have set up.

Narr. 2: Then Nebuchadnezzar was furious with Shadrach, Meshach and Abednego, and his attitude toward them changed.

Narr. 3: He ordered the furnace heated seven times hotter than usual and commanded some of the strongest soldiers in his army to tie up Shadrach, Meshach and Abednego and throw them into the blazing furnace.

Narr. 1: So these men, wearing their robes, trousers, turbans and other clothes, were bound and thrown into the blazing furnace.

Narr. 2: The king's command was so urgent and the furnace so hot that the flames of the fire killed the men who took up Shadrach, Meshach and Abednego, . . .

Narr. 3: And these three men, firmly tied, fell into the blazing furnace.

Narr. 1: Then King Nebuchadnezzar leaped to his feet in amazement and asked his advisers,

Nebuchadnezzar: Wasn't it three men that we tied up and threw into the fire?

Narr. 2: They replied, . . .

Astrologers 1 & 2: Certainly, O king.

Narr. 2: He said . . .

Nebuchadnezzar: Look! I see four men walking around in the fire, unbound and unharmed, and the fourth looks like a son of the gods.

Narr. 3: Nebuchadnezzar then approached the opening of the blazing furnace and shouted,

Nebuchadnezzar: Shadrach, Meshach, Abednego, servants of the Most High God, come out! Come here!

Narr. 1: So Shadrach, Meshach and Abednego came out of the fire,

Narr. 2: And the satraps, prefects, governors and royal visitors crowded around them.

Narr. 3: They saw that the fire had not harmed their bodies, nor was a hair on their heads singed;

Narr. 1: Their robes were not scorched,

Narr. 2: And there was no smell of fire on them.

Narr. 3: Then Nebuchadnezzar said,

Nebuchadnezzar: Praise be to the God of Shadrach, Meshach and Abednego, who has sent his angel and rescued his servants! They trusted in him and defied the king's command and were willing to give up their lives rather than serve or worship any god except their own God. Therefore, I decree that the people of any nation or language who say anything against the God of Shadrach, Meshach and Abednego be cut to pieces and their houses be turned into piles of rubble, for no other god can save in this way.

Narr. 1: Then the king promoted Shadrach, Meshach and Abednego in the province of Babylon.

All: Amen!

Daniel 3

The Faithful

LEADER: In response to a centurion's faith, Jesus said, "I tell you, I have not found such great faith even in Israel."

PEOPLE: Tell us; what is faith?

SOLO 1: Faith is being sure of what we hope for and certain of what we do not see.

LEADER: This is what the ancients were commended for.

PEOPLE: Who are those who were faithful?

LEADER: By faith Abel offered God a better sacrifice than Cain did.

SOLO 1: Abel kept flocks, and Cain worked the soil.

SOLO 2: In the course of time Cain brought some of the fruits of the soil as an offering to the Lord.

SOLO 1: But Abel brought fat portions from some of the firstborn of his flock.

LEADER: The Lord looked with favor on Abel and his offering, but on Cain and his offering he did not look with favor.

SOLO 2: So Cain was very angry.

LEADER: The the Lord said to Cain, "Why are you angry? Why is your face downcast? If you do what is right, will you not be accepted? Sin is crouching at your door; it desires to have you, but you must master it."

SOLO 2: But Cain attacked his brother Abel and killed him.

PEOPLE: Abel was the man of faith.

LEADER: By faith Enoch was taken from this life, so that he did not experience death.

SOLO 1: When Enoch had lived 65 years, he became the father of Methuselah.

SOLO 2: And after he became the father of Methuselah, Enoch walked with God . . .

SOLO 1: And then he was no more, because God took him away.

LEADER: But before he was taken, he was commended as one who pleased God.

PEOPLE: Without faith it is impossible to please God.

LEADER: By faith Noah, when warned about things not yet seen, in holy fear built an ark to save his family.

PEOPLE: By his faith he condemned the world and became heir of the righteousness that comes by faith.

SOLO 1: God said to Noah, "I am going to bring floodwaters on the earth to destroy all life under the heavens.

SOLO 2: But I will establish my covenant with you, and you will enter the ark—you and your sons and your wife and your sons' wives with you.

SOLO 1: You are to bring into the ark two of all living creatures, male and female."

LEADER: Noah did everything just as God commanded him.

SOLO 1: The Lord then said to Noah, "Go into the ark, you and your whole family, because I have found you righteous."

SOLO 2: And then the rain fell on the earth forty days and forty nights.

Solo 1: After forty days Noah opened the window he had made in the ark.

Solo 2: Then God said to Noah, "Come out of the ark."

Solo 1: So Noah built an altar to the Lord and he sacrificed burnt offerings on it.

Solo 2: The Lord smelled the pleasant aroma and said in his heart,

Leader: Never again will I curse the ground because of man. And never again will I destroy all living creatures, as I have done.

Solo 1: As long as the earth endures, seedtime and harvest, cold and heat,

Solo 2: Summer and winter, day and night will never cease.

Leader: Then God blessed Noah and his sons.

People: Noah was a man of faith.

Leader: By faith Abraham . . .

Solo 1: When called to go to a place he would later receive as his inheritance, obeyed and went, even though he did not know where he was going.

People: By faith Abraham . . .

Solo 2: Made his home in the promised land like a stranger in a foreign country.

People: By faith Abraham . . .

Solo 1: Was looking forward to the city with foundations, whose architect and builder is God.

All: By faith Abraham . . .

Solo 2: When God tested him, offered Isaac, his one and only son, as a sacrifice.

People: Abraham was a man of faith.

Leader: Men of faith—the roll call continues . . . By faith Isaac blessed Jacob and Esau in regard to their future.

Solo 1: By faith Jacob, when he was dying, blessed each of Joseph's sons.

Solo 2: By faith Joseph, when his end was near, spoke about the exodus of the Israelites from Egypt and gave instructions about his burial.

Solo 1: By faith Moses' parents hid him after he was born, because they saw he was no ordinary child, and they were not afraid of the king's edict.

Solo 2: By faith Moses, when he had grown up, refused to be known as the son of Pharaoh's daughter.

Solo 1: By faith he chose to be mistreated along with the people of God rather than to enjoy the pleasures of sin for a short time.

Solo 2: By faith he left Egypt, not fearing the king's anger; he persevered because he saw him who is invisable.

Solo 1: By faith the people passed through the Red Sea as on dry ground.

People: Moses was a man of faith.

Leader: And what more shall I say? There was . . .

Solo 1: Gideon . . .

Solo 2: Barak . . .

Solo 1: Samson . . .

Solo 2: Jephthah . . .

Solo 1: David . . .

Solo 2: Samuel and the prophets,

Leader: Who through faith conquered kingdoms,

Solo 1: Administered justice, and gained what was promised;

SOLO 2: Who shut the mouths of lions,

SOLO 1: Quenched the fury of the flames, and escaped the edge of the sword;

SOLO 2: Whose weakness was turned to strength;

SOLO 1: And who became powerful in battle and routed foreign armies.

ALL: All these were persons of faith.

LEADER: By faith women received back their dead, raised to life again.

SOLO 1: Others were tortured.

SOLO 2: Some faced jeers and flogging,

SOLO 1: While still others were chained and put in prison.

SOLO 2: They were stoned;

SOLO 1: They were sawed in two;

SOLO 2: They were put to death by the sword.

SOLO 1: They went about destitute, persecuted and mistreated—

LEADER: The world was not worthy of them.

PEOPLE: These were all commended for their faith.

ALL: These were all persons of faith.

LEADER: Therefore, since we have a great high priest, Jesus the Son of God, . . .

ALL: Let us hold firm to the faith we possess.

LUKE 7:9; HEBREWS 11:1-2, 4; GENESIS 4:2-8; HEBREWS 11:5; GENESIS 5:21-24; HEBREWS 11:5-7; GENESIS 6:17-19, 22; 7:1, 12; 8:6, 15, 20-22; 9:1; HEBREWS 11:8-10, 17, 20-25, 27, 29, 32-39; 4:14

■ *Gospel Narratives*

God with Us

LEADER: Come, let us adore him.

PEOPLE: Immanuel, God with us.

SOLO 1: The Lord himself will give you a sign: The virgin will be with child and will give birth to a son, and will call him Immanuel.

PEOPLE: God with us.

SOLO 2: But you, Bethlehem Ephrathah, though you are small among the clans of Judah, out of you will come for me one who will be ruler over Israel, whose origins are from of old, from ancient times.

PEOPLE: They will live securely.

SOLO 2: He will stand in the strength of the Lord.

PEOPLE: He will be their peace.

LEADER: In the sixth month, God sent the angel Gabriel to Nazareth, a town in Galilee, to a virgin pledged to be married to a man named Joseph, a descendant of David.

PEOPLE: The Virgin Mary.

SOLO 1: Greetings, you who are highly favored! The Lord is with you. Do not be afraid, Mary, you have found favor with God.

SOLO 3: I am the Lord's servant.

SOLO 1: You will be with child and give birth to a son, and you are to give him the name Jesus.

SOLO 2: He will shepherd his flock in the name of the Lord.

PEOPLE: They will live securely.

SOLO 1: He will be great and will be called the Son of the Most High.

SOLO 2: His greatness will reach to the ends of the earth.

PEOPLE: He will be their peace.

SOLO 1: The Lord God will give him the throne of his father David, and he will reign over the house of Jacob forever.

PEOPLE: His kingdom will never end.

SOLO 3: How will this be, since I am a virgin?

SOLO 1: The Holy Spirit will come upon you, and the power of the Most High will overshadow you. So the holy one to be born will be called the Son of God.

SOLO 3: I am the Lord's servant. May it be to me as you have said.

PEOPLE: For nothing is impossible with God.

ISAIAH 7:14; MICAH 5:2, 4-5; LUKE 1:26-38

To Us a Son Is Given

Narr. 1: In those days Caesar Augustus issued a decree that a census should be taken of the entire Roman world.

Narr. 2: And everyone went to his own town to register.

Narr. 1: So Joseph also went up from the town of Nazareth in Galilee to Judea, to Bethlehem the town of David, because he belonged to the house and line of David.

Narr. 2: He went to register with Mary, to whom he was pledged to be married and who was expecting a child.

Leader: Let the heavens rejoice, let the earth be glad.

People: Let the sea resound, and all that is in it.

Leader: Then all the trees of the forest will sing for joy.

People: Let the fields be jubilant, and everything in them.

Leader: They will sing before the Lord, for he comes,

People: He comes to judge the earth!

Leader: He will judge the world in righteousness.

People: He will judge the peoples in his truth.

Narr. 1: While they were there, the time came for the baby to be born, and she gave birth to her firstborn, a son.

Narr. 2: She wrapped him in cloths and placed him in a manger, because there was no room for them in the inn.

Leader: The people walking in darkness have seen a great light.

People: For to us a child is born.

Leader: On those living in a land of darkness—a light has dawned.

People: To us a son is given.

Narr. 1: And there were shepherds living out in the fields nearby, keeping watch over their flocks at night.

Narr. 2: An angel of the Lord appeared to them, and the glory of the Lord shone around them, and they were terrified.

Choir Women: Do not be afraid.

Choir Men: I bring you good news of great joy that will be for all the people.

Narr. 2: The angel said to them, "Today in the town of David a Savior has been born to you; he is Christ the Lord. This will be a sign to you: You will find a baby wrapped in cloths and lying in a manger."

Narr. 1: Suddenly a great company of the heavenly host appeared with the angel, praising God.

Choir: Glory to God in the highest, and on earth peace to men on whom his favor rests.

Leader: Sing to the Lord a new song;

People: Sing to the Lord, all the earth.

Leader: Sing to the Lord, praise his name;

People: Proclaim his salvation day after day.

Leader: Declare his glory among the nations.

PEOPLE: Ascribe to the Lord glory and strength.

LEADER: Splendor and majesty are before him.

PEOPLE: Ascribe to the Lord the glory due his name.

LEADER: Strength and glory are in his sanctuary.

PEOPLE: Worship the Lord in the splendor of his holiness.

LEADER: He will judge the peoples with equity.

PEOPLE: The Lord reigns!

NARR. 1: When the angels had left them and gone into heaven, the shepherds said to one another, "Let's go to Bethlehem and see this thing that has happened, which the Lord has told us about."

NARR. 2: So they hurried off and found Mary and Joseph, and the baby, who was lying in the manger.

NARR. 1: When they had seen him, they spread the word concerning what had been told them about this child,

CHOIR: And all who heard it were amazed.

NARR. 2: But Mary treasured up all these things and pondered them in her heart.

NARR. 1: For to us a child is born, to us a son is given,

NARR. 2: And the government will be on his shoulders.

LEADER: And he will be called Wonderful Counselor,

PEOPLE: Mighty God,

LEADER: Everlasting Father,

PEOPLE: Prince of Peace.

NARR. 1: Of the increase of his government and peace there will be no end.

NARR. 2: He will reign on David's throne and over his kingdom.

LEADER: He will reign with justice and righteousness from that time on and forever.

PEOPLE: The zeal of the Lord Almighty will accomplish this.

LUKE 2:1-19; PSALM 96; ISAIAH 9:2, 6-7

Gifts for a King

LEADER: Where is the one who has been born king of the Jews?

RIGHT: Jesus was born in Bethlehem in Judea.

LEFT: In Bethlehem in Judea, for this is what the prophet has written.

LEADER: But you, Bethlehem, in the land of Judea, are by no means least among the rulers of Judah; for out of you will come a ruler who will be the shepherd of my people Israel.

RIGHT: Arise, shine, for your light has come,

LEFT: And the glory of the Lord rises upon you.

LEADER: See, darkness covers the earth and thick darkness is over the peoples, but the Lord rises upon you and his glory appears over you.

RIGHT: Arise, shine, for your light has come,

LEFT: And the glory of the Lord rises upon you.

LEADER: Nations will come to your light, and kings to the brightness of your dawn.

RIGHT: Lift up your eyes and look about you:

LEFT: All assemble and come to you.

LEADER: During the time of King Herod, Magi from the east came to Jerusalem.

SOLO 1: The wealth on the seas will be brought to you.

SOLO 2: To you the riches of the nations will come.

LEADER: Magi from the east came to Jerusalem and asked, "Where is the one who has been born king of the Jews? We saw his star in the east and have come to worship him."

SOLO 1: All from Sheba will come, bearing gold and incense.

SOLO 2: All from Sheba will come, proclaiming the praise of the Lord.

LEADER: But you, Bethlehem, in the land of Judea, are by no means least among the rulers of Judah; for out of you will come a ruler who will be the shepherd of my people Israel.

PEOPLE: He will endure as long as the sun.

SOLO 1: He will judge your people in righteousness.

SOLO 2: The mountains will bring prosperity to the people.

PEOPLE: He will endure as long as the moon.

SOLO 1: He will judge your afflicted ones with justice.

SOLO 2: The hills will bring the fruit of righteousness.

PEOPLE: He will endure through all generations.

LEADER: And the star the Magi had seen in the east went ahead of them until it stopped over the place where the child was.

RIGHT: Arise, shine, for your light has come,

LEFT: And the glory of the Lord rises upon you.

Leader: On coming to the house, the Magi saw the child with his mother Mary, and they bowed down and worshiped him.

Right: Lift up your eyes and look about you:

Left: All assemble and come to you.

Leader: Then the Magi opened their treasures and presented him with gifts of gold and of incense and of myrrh.

Solo 1: The desert tribes will bow before him.

Solo 2: The kings of Tarshish and of distant shores will bring tribute to him.

Right: He will rule from sea to sea.

Left: He will rule to the ends of the earth.

Solo 1: The kings of Sheba and Seba will present him gifts.

Solo 2: All kings will bow down to him and all nations will serve him.

Right: He will rule from sea to sea.

Left: He will rule to the ends of the earth.

Solo 1: For he will deliver the needy who cry out,

Solo 2: He will deliver the afflicted who have no one to help.

People: Precious is their blood in his sight.

Solo 1: He will take pity on the weak and the needy and save the needy from death.

Solo 2: He will rescue them from oppression and violence.

People: Precious is their blood in his sight.

Matthew 2:1-11; Isaiah 60:1-6;
Psalm 72:1-14

Christ's Mission

LEADER: Jesus went to Nazareth, where he had been brought up.

CHOIR: On the Sabbath day he went into the synagogue, as was the custom.

LEADER: And he stood up to read.

CHOIR: The Spirit of the Lord is on me,

PEOPLE: Because he has anointed me to preach good news to the poor.

LEADER: He has sent me to preach freedom for the prisoners

PEOPLE: And recovery of sight for the blind,

CHOIR: To release the oppressed,

PEOPLE: To proclaim the year of the Lord's favor.

LEADER: And he began by saying to them,

CHOIR: Today this scripture is fulfilled in your hearing.

LEADER: If your enemy is hungry,

PEOPLE: Feed him;

LEADER: If he is thirsty,

PEOPLE: Give him something to drink.

CHOIR: Do not be overcome by evil,

ALL: But overcome evil with good.

LUKE 4:16, 18-19, 21; ROMANS 12:20-21

The Prophet in His Hometown

SOLO 1: And he began by saying to them, "Today this scripture is fulfilled in your hearing."

CHOIR: Isn't this Joseph's son?

SOLO 1: All spoke well of him and were amazed at the gracious words that came from his lips.

CHOIR: Is this the son of Joseph?

SOLO 2: Surely you will quote this proverb to me: "Physician, heal yourself!"

CHOIR: Do here in your hometown what we have heard that you did in Capernaum.

SOLO 2: I tell you the truth, no prophet is accepted in his hometown.

CHOIR: Isn't this Joseph's son?

SOLO 1: I assure you that there were many widows in Israel in Elijah's time, when the sky was shut for three and a half years and there was a severe famine throughout the land.

Solo 2: Yet Elijah was not sent to any of them, but to a widow in the region of Sidon.

Solo 3: And there were many in Israel with leprosy in the time of Elisha the prophet,

Solo 4: Yet not one of them was cleansed—only Naaman the Syrian.

Solo 3: Now Naaman was commander of the army of the king of Aram.

Solo 4: He was a great man in the sight of his master and highly regarded, because through him the Lord had given victory to Aram.

Solo 3: He was a valiant soldier, but he had leprosy.

Solo 4: There were many in Israel with leprosy—yet only Naaman was cleansed—Naaman, the Syrian.

Solo 3: All the people in the synagogue were furious when they heard this.

Choir: Isn't this Joseph's son?

Solo 4: They got up, drove him out of the town, and took him to the brow of the hill on which the town was built, in order to throw him down the cliff.

Solo 1: But he walked right through the crowd and went on his way.

Choir: Was this the son of Joseph?

Luke 4:21-30; 2 Kings 5:1

The Man Born Blind

Narr. 1: As he went along, he saw a man blind from birth.

Narr. 2: His disciples asked him, "Rabbi, who sinned, this man or his parents, that he was born blind?"

Solo 1: Neither this man nor his parents sinned, but this happened so that the work of God might be displayed in his life. As long as it is day, we must do the work of him who sent me.

People: Night is coming, when no one can work.

Solo 1: While I am in the world, I am the light of the world.

People: The true light that gives light to every man.

Narr. 1: Having said this, he spit on the ground, made some mud with the saliva, and put it on the man's eyes.

Solo 1: Go, wash in the Pool of Siloam.

Narr. 2: So the man went and washed, and came home seeing.

Narr. 1: His neighbors and those who had formerly seen him begging asked, "Isn't this the same man who used to sit and beg?"

Narr. 2: Some claimed that he was.

Narr. 1: Others said, "No, he only looks like him."

Narr. 2: But he himself insisted, "I am the man."

Solo 2: I am the man!

People: How then were your eyes opened?

Solo 2: The man they call Jesus made some mud and put it on my eyes. He told me to go to Siloam and wash. So I went and washed, and then I could see.

People: Where is this man?

Solo 2: I don't know.

Narr. 1: They brought to the Pharisees the man who had been blind. Now the day on which Jesus had made the mud and opened the man's eyes was a Sabbath.

Narr. 2: Therefore the Pharisees also asked him how he had received his sight.

Solo 2: He put mud on my eyes, and I washed, and now I see.

Narr. 1: Some of the Pharisees said, "This man is not from God."

People: He does not keep the Sabbath!

Narr. 1: But others asked, "How can a sinner do such miraculous signs?" So they were divided.

Narr. 2: Finally they turned again to the blind man,

Right: What have you to say about him?

Left: It was your eyes he opened.

Solo 2: He is a prophet.

Narr. 1: The Jews still did not believe that he had been blind and had received his sight until they sent for the man's parents.

Right: Is this your son?

Left: Is this the one you say was born blind?

People: How is it that now he can see?

Men: We know he is our son.

Women: We know he was born blind.

Men: But how he can see now, or who opened his eyes, we don't know.

Women: Ask him. He is of age; he will speak for himself.

Narr. 1: His parents said this because they were afraid of the Jews,

Narr. 2: For already the Jews had decided that anyone who acknowledged that Jesus was the Christ would be put out of the synagogue.

Narr. 1: That was why his parents said, "He is of age; ask him."

Narr. 2: A second time they summoned the man who had been blind.

Right: Give glory to God.

Left: We know this man is a sinner.

Solo 2: Whether he is a sinner or not, I don't know. One thing I do know. I was blind but now I see!

Right: What did he do to you?

Left: How did he open your eyes?

Solo 2: I have told you already and you did not listen. Why do you want to hear it again? Do you want to become his disciples, too?

Right: You are this fellow's disciple!

Left: We are disciples of Moses!

Right: We know that God spoke to Moses,

Left: But as for this fellow, we don't even know where he comes from!

Solo 2: Now that is remarkable! You don't know where he comes from, yet he opened my eyes. We know that God does not listen to sinners. He listens to the godly man who does his will.

Choir: You were steeped in sin at birth!

Solo 2: Nobody has ever heard of opening the eyes of a man born blind. If this man were not from God, he could do nothing!

Choir: How dare you lecture us!

Narr. 1: And they threw him out.

Narr. 2: When he heard that they had thrown the blind man out, Jesus went to find him.

Solo 1: Do you believe in the Son of Man?

Solo 2: Who is he, sir? Tell me so that I may believe in him.

Solo 1: You have now seen him; in fact, he is the one speaking with you.

Solo 2: Lord, I believe.

Solo 1: For judgment I have come into this world, so that the blind will see and those who see will become blind.

Narr. 1: For you were once darkness.

People: Now we are light in the Lord.

Narr. 2: The fruit of the light consists in all goodness, righteousness and truth.

Right: We will live as children of light,

Left: And find out what pleases the Lord.

Narr. 1: Have nothing to do with the fruitless deeds of darkness.

People: We will expose them.

Narr. 2: Everything exposed by the light becomes visible.

People: It is light that makes everything visible.

John 1:9; 9:1-39; Ephesians 5:8-14

Life Comes to Dry Bones

LEADER: The hand of the Lord was upon me, and he brought me out by the Spirit of the Lord and set me in the middle of a valley.

PEOPLE: It was full of bones.

LEADER: He led me back and forth among them, and I saw a great many bones on the floor of the valley.

PEOPLE: Bones that were very dry.

LEADER: The Lord asked me, "Son of man, can these bones live?"

PEOPLE: O Sovereign Lord, you alone know.

LEADER: Then he said to me, "Prophesy to these bones and say to them, 'Dry bones, hear the word of the Lord!'"

PEOPLE: Our bones are dried up and our hope is gone; we are cut off.

LEADER: This is what the Sovereign Lord says to these bones:

CHOIR: I will make breath enter you, and you will come to life.

LEADER: I will attach tendons to you and make flesh come upon you and cover you with skin;

CHOIR: I will put breath in you, and you will come to life.

NARR. 1: Now a man named Lazarus was sick.

NARR. 2: He was from Bethany, the village of Mary and her sister Martha.

NARR. 1: This Mary, whose brother Lazarus now lay sick, was the same one who poured perfume on the Lord and wiped his feet with her hair.

NARR. 2: So the sisters sent word to Jesus, "Lord, the one you love is sick." When he heard this, Jesus said,

SOLO 1: This sickness will not end in death. No, it is for God's glory so that God's Son may be glorified through it.

NARR. 1: Jesus loved Martha and her sister and Lazarus.

NARR. 2: Yet when he heard that Lazarus was sick, he stayed where he was two more days. Then he said to his disciples,

SOLO 1: Let us go back to Judea.

CHOIR: But Rabbi, a short while ago the Jews tried to stone you, and yet you are going back there?

SOLO 1: Are there not twelve hours of daylight? A man who walks by day will not stumble, for he sees by this world's light. It is when he walks by night that he stumbles, for he has no light.

NARR. 2: After he had said this, he went on to tell them,

SOLO 1: Our friend Lazarus has fallen asleep; but I am going there to wake him up.

CHOIR: Lord, if he sleeps, he will get better.

NARR. 1: Jesus had been speaking of his death, but his disciples thought he meant natural sleep.

NARR. 2: So then he told them plainly,

SOLO 1: Lazarus is dead, and for your sake I am glad I was not there, so that you may believe. But let us go to him.

Narr. 1: Then Thomas (called Didymus) said to the rest of the disciples,

Narr. 2: Let us also go, that we may die with him.

Narr. 1: On his arrival, Jesus found that Lazarus had already been in the tomb for four days.

Narr. 2: Bethany was less than two miles from Jerusalem, and many Jews had come to Martha and Mary to comfort them in the loss of their brother.

Narr. 1: When Martha heard that Jesus was coming, she went out to meet him, but Mary stayed at home.

Solo 2: Lord, if you had been here, my brother would not have died. But I know that even now God will give you whatever you ask.

Solo 1: Your brother will rise again.

Solo 2: I know he will rise again in the resurrection at the last day.

Solo 1: I am the resurrection and the life. He who believes in me will live, even though he dies; and whoever lives and believes in me will never die. Do you believe this?

Solo 2: Yes, Lord, I believe that you are the Christ, the Son of God, who was to come into the world.

Narr. 2: And after she had said this, she went back and called her sister Mary aside.

Solo 2: The Teacher is here and is asking for you.

Narr. 1: When Mary heard this, she got up quickly and went to him.

Narr. 2: Now Jesus had not yet entered the village, but was still at the place where Martha had met him.

Narr. 1: When the Jews who had been with Mary in the house, comforting her, noticed how quickly she got up and went out, they followed her, supposing she was going to the tomb to mourn there.

Narr. 2: When Mary reached the place where Jesus was and saw him, she fell at his feet and said,

Solo 3: Lord, if you had been here, my brother would not have died.

Narr. 1: When Jesus saw her weeping, and the Jews who had come along with her also weeping, he was deeply moved in spirit and troubled.

Solo 1: Where have you laid him?

Solo 3: Come and see, Lord.

Narr. 2: Jesus wept.

Choir: How Jesus loved Lazarus!

Narr. 1: Jesus wept.

Narr. 2: Could not he who opened the eyes of the blind man have kept this man from dying?

Narr. 1: Jesus, once more deeply moved, came to the tomb.

Narr. 2: It was a cave with a stone laid across the entrance.

Solo 1: Take away the stone.

Solo 2: But, Lord, by this time there is a bad odor, for he has been there four days.

Solo 1: Did I not tell you that if you believed, you would see the glory of God?

Narr. 2: So they took away the stone. Then Jesus looked up and said,

Solo 1: Father, I thank you that you have heard me. I knew that you always hear me, but I said this for the benefit of the people standing here, that they may believe that you sent me.

Narr. 2: When he had said this, Jesus called in a loud voice,

Solo 1: Lazarus, come out!

Narr. 2: The dead man came out, his hands and feet wrapped with strips of linen, and a cloth around his face. Jesus said to them,

Solo 1: Take off the grave clothes and let him go.

Narr. 2: Therefore many of the Jews who had come to visit Mary, and had seen what Jesus did, put their faith in him.

Leader: And the bones came together,

Choir: Bone to bone.

Leader: I looked, and tendons and flesh appeared on them and skin covered them,

Choir: But there was no breath in them.

Leader: Come from the four winds, O breath, and breathe into these slain, that they may live.

Choir: And breath entered them.

Leader: I am going to open your graves,

Choir: And bring you up from them.

Leader: When I open your graves and bring you up from them,

Choir: I will put my Spirit in you and you will live.

John 11:1-45; Ezekiel 37:1-14

In Remembrance of Me

Narr. 1: It was just before the Passover Feast. Jesus knew that the time had come for him to leave this world and go to the Father.

Narr. 2: Having loved his own who were in the world, he now showed them the full extent of his love.

Narr. 1: The evening meal was being served, and the devil had already prompted Judas Iscariot, son of Simon, to betray Jesus.

Narr. 2: Jesus knew that the Father had put all things under his power, and that he had come from God and was returning to God; so he got up from the meal, took off his outer clothing, and wrapped a towel around his waist.

Narr. 1: After that, he poured water into a basin and began to wash his disciples' feet, drying them with the towel that was wrapped around him.

Narr. 2: He came to Simon Peter, who said to him,

Solo 2: Lord, are you going to wash my feet?

Solo 1: You do not realize now what I am doing, but later you will understand.

Solo 2: No, you shall never wash my feet.

Solo 1: Unless I wash you, you have no part with me.

Solo 2: Then, Lord, not just my feet but my hands and my head as well!

Solo 1: A person who has had a bath needs only to wash his feet; his whole body is clean. And you are clean, though not every one of you.

Narr. 1: For he knew who was going to betray him, and that was why he said not every one was clean.

Narr. 2: When he had finished washing their feet, he put on his clothes and returned to his place.

Solo 1: Do you understand what I have done for you?

Narr. 1: The Lord Jesus, on the night he was betrayed, took bread,

Solo 1: You call me "Teacher" and "Lord," and rightly so, for that is what I am.

Narr. 2: And when he had given thanks, he broke it.

Solo 1: Now that I, your Lord and Teacher, have washed your feet, you also should wash one another's feet.

Narr. 1: And he said, "This is my body, which is for you; do this in remembrance of me."

Solo 1: I have set you an example that you should do as I have done for you.

Narr. 2: In the same way, after supper he took the cup, saying, "This cup is the new covenant in my blood; do this, whenever you drink it, in remembrance of me."

Solo 1: For I received from the Lord what I also passed on to you.

Narr. 1: For whenever you eat this bread and drink this cup, you proclaim the Lord's death until he comes.

John 13:1-15; 1 Corinthians 11:23-26

Who Is My Accuser?

Solo 1: The Sovereign Lord has given me an instructed tongue, to know the word that sustains the weary.

Solo 2: He wakens me morning by morning.

Solo 1: He wakens my ear to listen like one being taught.

Solo 2: The Sovereign Lord has opened my ears, and I have not been rebellious; I have not drawn back.

Solo 1: I offered my back to those who beat me, my cheeks to those who pulled out my beard;

Solo 2: I did not hide my face from mocking and spitting.

Choir: Because the Sovereign Lord helps me, I will not be disgraced.

Solo 1: Therefore have I set my face like flint.

Solo 2: I know I will not be put to shame.

Choir: He who vindicates me is near.

Solo 1: "He who shares my bread has lifted up his heel against me." I am telling you this before it happens, so that when it does happen you will believe that I am He.

Narr. 2: After he had said this, Jesus was troubled in spirit and testified,

Solo 2: I tell you the truth, one of you is going to betray me.

Narr. 1: His disciples stared at one another, at a loss to know which of them he meant.

Narr. 2: One of them, the disciple whom Jesus loved, was reclining next to him.

Narr. 1: Simon Peter motioned to this disciple and said, "Ask him which one he means."

Narr. 2: Leaning back against Jesus, he asked him, "Lord, who is it?"

Solo 1: It is the one to whom I will give this piece of bread when I have dipped it in the dish.

Narr. 1: Then, dipping the piece of bread, he gave it to Judas Iscariot, son of Simon.

Narr. 2: As soon as Judas took the bread, Satan entered into him.

Solo 2: What you are about to do, do quickly.

Narr. 1: But no one at the meal understood why Jesus said this to him.

Narr. 2: Since Judas had charge of the money, some thought Jesus was telling him to buy what was needed for the Feast, or to give something to the poor.

Narr. 1: As soon as Judas had taken the bread, he went out.

Narr. 2: And it was night.

Solo 1: Who then will bring charges against me?

Solo 2: Let us face each other!

Solo 1: Who is my accuser?

Solo 2: Let him confront me!

Choir: It is the Sovereign Lord who helps me.

Solo 1: Who is he that will condemn me?

Solo 2: They will all wear out like a garment; the moths will eat them up.

Choir: O Lord, come quickly to help me.

Solo 1: May those who seek my life be put to shame and confusion.

Solo 2: May all who desire my ruin be turned back in disgrace.

Solo 1: But may all who seek you rejoice and be glad in you.

Solo 2: May those who love your salvation always say, "Let God be exalted!"

Choir: Let God be exalted!

Isaiah 50:4-9; John 13:18-30;
Psalm 70:1-4

The King of the Jews

Narr. 1: Jesus stood before Pilate. Pilate asked him, "Are you the king of the Jews?" "Yes, it is as you say," Jesus replied.

Narr. 2: When he was accused by the chief priests and the elders, he gave no answer.

Solo 1: Be merciful to me, O Lord, for I am in distress; my eyes grow weak with sorrow, my soul and my body with grief.

Solo 2: My life is consumed by anguish and my years by groaning; my strength fails because of my affliction, my bones grow weak.

Narr. 1: Then Pilate asked him, "Don't you hear the testimony they are bringing against you?"

Narr. 2: But Jesus made no reply, not even to a single charge—to the great amazement of the governor.

Solo 1: Because of all my enemies, I am the utter contempt of my neighbors;

Solo 2: I am a dread to my friends—

Solo 1: I am forgotten by them as though I were dead.

Solo 2: I have become like broken pottery.

Narr. 1: Now it was the governor's custom at the Feast to release a prisoner chosen by the crowd.

Narr. 2: At that time they had a notorious prisoner, called Barabbas.

Narr. 1: So when the crowd had gathered, Pilate asked them, "Which one do you want me to release to you: Barabbas, or Jesus who is called Christ?"

Narr. 2: For he knew it was out of envy that they had handed Jesus over to him.

Narr. 1: While Pilate was sitting on the judge's seat, his wife sent him this message: "Don't have anything to do with that innocent man, for I have suffered a great deal today in a dream because of him."

NARR. 2: But the chief priests and the elders persuaded the crowd to ask for Barabbas and to have Jesus executed.

SOLO 1: I hear the slander of many.

SOLO 2: There is terror on every side—

SOLO 1: They conspire against me and plot to take my life.

SOLO 2: There is terror on every side.

NARR. 1: Which of the two do you want me to release to you?

CHOIR: Barabbas.

NARR. 1: What shall I do, then, with Jesus who is called Christ?

CHOIR: Crucify him!

NARR. 1: Why? What crime has he committed?

CHOIR: Crucify him!

NARR. 2: When Pilate saw that he was getting nowhere, but that instead an uproar was starting, he took water and washed his hands in front of the crowd.

NARR. 1: I am innocent of this man's blood; it is your responsibility!

CHOIR: Let his blood be on us and on our children!

MATTHEW 27:11-25; PSALM 31:9-13

It Is Finished

NARR. 1: Jesus carried his own cross to the place of the Skull.

NARR. 2: Jesus carried his cross to Golgotha.

NARR. 1: Here they crucified him with two others—

NARR. 2: One on each side and Jesus in the middle.

SOLO 1: Why are you so far from saving me, so far from the words of my groaning?

SOLO 2: O my God, I cry out by day, but you do not answer, by night, and am not silent.

CHOIR: My God, my God, why have you forsaken me?

SOLO 1: Yet you are enthroned as the Holy One; you are the praise of Israel. In you our fathers put their trust; they trusted and you delivered them.

SOLO 2: They cried to you and were saved; in you they trusted and were not disappointed.

NARR. 1: Pilate had a notice prepared and fastened to the cross.

NARR. 2: It read: JESUS OF NAZARETH, THE KING OF THE JEWS.

Narr. 1: Many of the Jews read this sign, for the place where Jesus was crucified was near the city.

Narr. 2: The chief priests of the Jews protested to Pilate, "Do not write 'The King of the Jews.'"

Narr. 1: Many read this sign, which was written in Aramaic, Latin and Greek.

Narr. 2: Pilate answered, "What I have written, I have written."

Narr. 1: Do not write "The King of the Jews," but that this man claimed to be king of the Jews.

Narr. 2: What I have written, I have written.

Solo 1: All who see me mock me; they hurl insults, shaking their heads:

Solo 2: He trusts in the Lord; let the Lord rescue him. Let him deliver him, since he delights in him.

Choir: My God, my God, why have you forsaken me?

Solo 1: Yet you brought me out of the womb; you made me trust in you even at my mother's breast.

Solo 2: From birth I was cast upon you; from my mother's womb you have been my God.

Narr. 1: The soldiers crucified Jesus.

Narr. 2: They took his clothes.

Narr. 1: The soldiers divided his clothes into four shares.

Narr. 2: They each had a share with the undergarment remaining.

Narr. 1: "Let's not tear it," they said.

Narr. 2: Let's decide by lot who will get it.

Solo 1: My heart has turned to wax; it has melted away within me.

Solo 2: I am poured out like water, and all my bones are out of joint.

Choir: Do not be far from me, for trouble is near.

Solo 1: My strength is dried up like a potsherd, and my tongue sticks to the roof of my mouth;

Solo 2: You lay me in the dust of death.

Choir: There is no one to help.

Solo 1: Dogs have surrounded me; a band of evil men has encircled me,

Solo 2: They have pierced my hands and my feet.

Solo 1: I can count all my bones; people stare and gloat over me.

Solo 2: They divide my garments among them and cast lots for my clothing.

Narr. 1: Jesus knew all was now completed.

Narr. 2: Jesus said, "I am thirsty."

Narr. 1: They soaked a sponge in a jar of wine vinegar.

Narr. 2: They put the sponge on a stalk of the hyssop plant.

Narr. 1: They lifted the sponge to Jesus' lips.

Narr. 2: Jesus said, "It is finished."

Narr. 1: With that, he bowed his head and gave up his spirit.

Narr. 2: It is finished.

John 19:17-30; Psalm 22

We Have Seen the Lord

Narr.: On the evening of that first day of the week, when the disciples were together, with the doors locked for fear of the Jews,

Solo 1: Jesus came and stood among them and said, "Peace be with you!"

Narr.: After he said this, he showed them his hands and side.

Choir: The disciples were overjoyed when they saw the Lord.

Narr.: Again Jesus said, "Peace be with you! As the Father has sent me, I am sending you."

Solo 1: And with that he breathed on them and said, "Receive the Holy Spirit.

Solo 2: If you forgive anyone his sins, they are forgiven;

Solo 3: If you do not forgive them, they are not forgiven."

Narr.: Now Thomas (called Didymus), one of the Twelve, was not with the disciples when Jesus came.

Solo 1: So the other disciples told him, "We have seen the Lord!"

Solo 4: But he said to them, "Unless I see the nail marks in his hands and put my finger where the nails were, and put my hand into his side, I will not believe it."

Narr.: A week later his disciples were in the house again, and Thomas was with them.

Solo 1: Though the doors were locked, Jesus came and stood among them and said, "Peace be with you!"

Solo 4: Then he said to Thomas, "Put your finger here; see my hands. Reach out your hand and put it into my side.

Choir: Stop doubting and believe."

Solo 1: Thomas said to him, "My Lord and my God!"

Narr.: Then Jesus told him, "Because you have seen me, you have believed; blessed are those who have not seen and yet have believed."

Choir: All the believers were one in heart and mind.

Solo 2: How good and pleasant it is when brothers live together in unity!

Solo 3: It is like precious oil poured on the head, running down on the beard, running down on Aaron's beard, down upon the collar of his robes.

Choir: All the believers were one in heart and mind.

Narr.: No one claimed that any of his possessions was his own, but they shared everything they had.

Solo 2: How good and pleasant it is when brothers live together in unity!

Solo 3: It is as if the dew of Hermon were falling on Mount Zion. For there the Lord bestows his blessing, even life forevermore.

Narr.: With great power the apostles continued to testify to the resurrection of the Lord Jesus, and much grace was upon them all.

Choir: All the believers were one in heart and mind.

John 20:19-29; Acts 4:32-33; Psalm 133

The Emmaus Road Incident

NARR. 1: On an Easter Sunday, when daylight slowly gave way to eventide . . .

NARR. 2: On a much-traveled road between Jerusalem and Emmaus . . .

NARR. 1: Two sorrowing men relived the events of that dark day, not knowing that it was—

NARRS. 1 & 2: Resurrection Day!

MAN 1: Remember how he said, "I will never leave you or forsake you"?

MAN 2: Remember when he said, "I am the way, the truth, and the life"?

MAN 1: Remember where he said, "Lift up your heads, because your redemption is drawing near"?

NARR. 1: As the two disciples talked with each other about everything that had happened . . .

NARR. 2: As they talked and discussed these things with each other—

NARR. 1: Jesus himself came up and walked along with them.

NARR. 2: But they were kept from recognizing him. He asked them,

NARR. 3: What are you discussing together?

MAN 1: Are you only a visitor to Jerusalem and do not know the things that have happened there in these days?

NARR. 3: What things?

BOTH MEN: About Jesus of Nazareth.

MAN 1: He was a prophet,

MAN 2: Powerful in word and deed before God and all the people.

MAN 1: The chief priests and our rulers handed him over to be sentenced to death . . .

MAN 2: And they crucified him!

MAN 1: We hoped that he was the one who was going to redeem Israel.

MAN 2: And what is more, it is the third day since all this took place.

MAN 1: In addition, some of our women gave us amazing news.

MAN 2: They went to the tomb early this morning but didn't find his body.

MAN 1: They told us that they had seen a vision of angels, who said he was alive.

MAN 2: Some of our companions went to the tomb, but they did not see him.

NARR. 1: Then Jesus said to them . . .

NARR. 3: How foolish you are, and how slow of heart to believe all that the prophets have spoken! Did not the Christ have to suffer these things and then enter his glory?

NARR. 2: Then beginning with Moses and all the Prophets, he explained to them what was said in the Scripture concerning himself.

NARR. 1: As they approached the village, Jesus acted as if he were going farther.

NARR. 2: The two men still did not recognize Jesus but strongly urged him,

MAN 1: Stay with us.

MAN 2: Yes, it's nearly evening; the day is almost over.

NARR. 2: So he went in to stay with them.

NARR. 1: When he was at the table with them, he took bread, gave thanks, broke it and gave it to them.

NARR. 2: Then their eyes were opened,

NARRS. 1 & 2: They recognized Jesus!

BOTH MEN: It is the Lord!

NARR. 2: And then he disappeared from their sight.

MAN 1: It was the Lord!

MAN 2: It was Jesus.

BOTH MEN: Were not our hearts burning within us while he talked with us?

ALL: It is true! The Lord has risen!

LUKE 24:13-34

The Day of Pentecost

Leader: When the day of Pentecost came, they were all together in one place, as Jesus had commanded—

People: Stay in the city until you have been clothed with power from on high.

Leader: It was Jesus who promised One who would be with his followers after he was gone.

People: If you love me, you will obey what I have commanded.

Leader: And I will ask the Father, and he will give you another Counselor to be with you forever—

Choir: The Spirit of Truth.

Leader: The world cannot accept him,

Men: Because it neither sees him nor knows him.

Women: But we know him, for he lives with us

Men: And will be in us.

Leader: Jesus said, "I will not leave you as orphans;

Choir: I will come to you."

Leader: So, when the day of Pentecost came,

People: They were all together in one place.

Choir: Suddenly a sound like the blowing of a violent wind came from heaven and filled the whole house where they they were sitting.

Women: They saw what seemed to be tongues of fire that separated and came to rest on each of them.

Choir: And they began to speak in other tongues as the Spirit enabled them.

All: All of them were filled with the Holy Spirit.

Leader: In the last days, God says, I will pour out my Spirit on all people.

Women: Your sons and daughters will prophesy,

Men: Your young men will see visions,

Choir: Your old men will dream dreams.

Leader: Even on my servants, both men and women, I will pour out my Spirit.

People: And everyone who calls on the name of the Lord will be saved.

Acts 2:1-4, 17-18, 21; Luke 24:49; John 14:15-18

Stephen

Narr. 1: This is the story of Stephen, a man full of faith, God's grace, power, and the Holy Spirit.

Narr. 2: This is a story that begins in Jerusalem in the days when the number of disciples was rapidly on the increase,

Narr. 1: When the Grecian Jews among them complained against the Hebraic Jews because their widows were being overlooked in the daily distribution of the food.

Narr. 2: So the Twelve gathered all the disciples together and said, . . .

Solo 1: It would not be right for us to neglect the ministry of the word of God in order to wait on tables.

Solo 2: Brothers, choose seven men from among you who are known to be full of the Spirit and wisdom.

Solo 3: We will turn this responsibility over to them.

Solo 1: Good. And we'll give our attention to prayer and the ministry of the word.

Narr. 2: This proposal pleased the whole group. So the selection process began.

Solo 1: So, who shall we select?

Solo 2: I say they should all be Greek.

Solo 3: Then I nominate Nicanor.

Solo 2: And I select Timon and Parmenas.

Solo 1: And don't forget Nicolas from Antioch.

Solo 3: I nominate Stephen. We all know him to be a man full of faith and the Holy Spirit.

Narr. 1: The group then presented these five men to the apostles, who prayed and laid their hands on them.

Narr. 2: So the word of God spread and the number of disciples in Jerusalem increased rapidly.

Narr. 1: Giving leadership to much of the growth was Stephen, a man full of God's grace and power. He did great wonders and miraculous signs among the people.

Narr. 2: In the midst of such success opposition arose from Jewish members of what was called the Synagogue of Freedmen.

Narr. 1: The men of the synagogue argued with Stephen, but they could not stand up against his wisdom . . .

Narr. 2: Or the Spirit by whom he spoke.

Narr. 1: So they secretly persuaded some men to make charges against Stephen.

Solo 1: I have heard Stephen speak words of blasphemy.

Solo 2: I've heard him blaspheme Moses!

Solo 3: And I have heard him speak blasphemy against God himself.

Solos 1 & 2: No! Not against God!

Solo 3: Against God!

Solo 1: I say bring him up to the Sanhedrin for trial.

Narr. 1: So the people and the elders and the teachers of the law seized Stephen and brought him before the Sanhedrin.

NARR. 2: Then came in the false witnesses.

SOLO 2: The man Stephen never stops speaking against this holy place and against the law!

SOLO 3: We have heard him say that the dead Jesus of Nazareth will destroy our temple!

SOLO 1: I heard him say that the dead Jesus will do away with the customs Moses handed down to us!

NARR. 1: Then suddenly, as all who were sitting in the Sanhedrin looked intently at Stephen, they saw that . . .

SOLOS 1, 2 & 3 *(with awe):* His face was like the face of an angel!

NARR. 2: Then the high priest asked him,

SOLO 1: Are these charges true?

NARR. 2: There was a long silence, and then Stephen stood and replied . . .

SOLO 2: Brothers and fathers, listen to me . . .

NARR. 2: So began Stephen's defense to the Sanhedrin.

SOLO 2: The God of glory appeared to our father Abraham while he was still in Mesopotamia. It was God who said, "Leave your country and your people, and go to the land I will show you."

NARR. 2: Stephen continued with an inspired retelling of Hebrew history from Abraham, Joseph, Moses, to Solomon. Finally, he brought his message home . . .

SOLO 2: You stiff-necked people with uncircumcised hearts and ears! You are just like your fathers: You always resist the Holy Spirit! Was there ever a prophet your fathers did not persecute? They even killed those who predicted the coming of the Righteous One. And now you have betrayed and murdered him—you who have received the law that was put into effect through angels, but have not obeyed it.

NARR. 1: When the Sanhedrin heard these words, they were furious.

NARR. 2: They gnashed their teeth at him.

NARR. 1: But Stephen, full of the Holy Spirit, looked up to heaven and with the glow of paradise on his face, exclaimed . . .

SOLO 2: Look, I see heaven open, and the Son of Man is standing at the right hand of God.

NARR. 2: At this they covered their ears and yelled at the top of their voices . . .

SOLOS 1 & 3: Blasphemer! . . . Away with this man! . . . Stone him!

NARR. 1: So cowardly but desperate men dragged Stephen out of the city to stone him.

NARR. 2: The angry crowd removed their coats and threw them at the feet of a young man named Saul. He was from Tarsus.

NARR. 1: Then they picked up stones and began the prescribed execution for blasphemy.

SOLOS 1 & 3 *(overlapping each other):* This will quiet his profane mouth! . . . Kill him! . . . Silence his blaspheming!

NARR. 2: Without so much as a trial, Stephen was being executed for sharing his faith and the words of his Master.

SOLOS 1 & 3: Stone him! . . . Kill him! . . . Quiet his Christian tongue!

NARR. 1: And then the bleeding Stephen pulled himself up and tried to stand.

SOLO 1: Listen, he's going to speak!

Solo 2: Lord, do not hold this sin against them.

Narr. 1: Then Stephen fell to his knees and through bloodied lips prayed . . .

Solo 2: Lord Jesus, receive my spirit.

Narr. 2: With that, Stephen, a man full of faith, grace, power, and the Holy Spirit, gave up his life.

All: Remember, "He who loses his life for my sake will find it."

Narr. 1: A transfixed Saul was still there. He saw it all. By his silence he gave approval to the young man's martyrdom. And then he walked away.

Narr. 2: Godly men buried Stephen and mourned deeply for him.

Narr. 1: From that day a great persecution broke out against the church at Jerusalem.

Narr. 2: Saul was at the heart of this persecution. It was his desire to destroy the church.

Narr. 1: It was his wish to destroy the Lord's disciples.

Narr. 2: There is no doubt that in Saul's mind burned a picture of a young man filled with faith, grace, power, and God's Holy Spirit.

Narr. 1: Then came a day on a road to Damascus, that a light from heaven flashed through the clouds down to where Saul was.

Narr. 2: As if dead he fell to the ground, and a voice spoke to him,

Solo 1: Saul, Saul, why do you persecute me?

Solo 2: Who are you, Lord?

Solo 1: I am Jesus, whom you are persecuting.

Narr. 1: Then, according to God's plan, in three days, Saul of Tarsus became Paul, a chosen instrument to carry the name of Christ to the Gentiles and their kings.

Narr. 2: Paul grew in the Spirit and in power. He baffled the Jews by proving that Jesus is the Christ.

Narr. 1: And he vindicated the death of one Stephen, a man full of faith, grace, power, and God's Holy Spirit.

From Acts 6—9

Philip and the Ethiopian

Narr. 1: Now an angel of the Lord said to Philip, "Go south to the road—the desert road—that goes down from Jerusalem to Gaza."

Narr. 2: So he started out, and on his way he met an Ethiopian eunuch, an important official in charge of all the treasury of Candace, queen of the Ethiopians.

Narr. 1: This man had gone to Jerusalem to worship, and on his way home was sitting in his chariot reading the book of Isaiah the prophet.

Narr. 2: The Spirit told Philip, "Go to that chariot and stay near it."

Narr. 1: Then Philip ran up to the chariot and heard the man reading Isaiah the prophet.

Solo 1: Do you understand what you are reading?

Solo 2: How can I, unless someone explains it to me?

Narr. 1: So he invited Philip to come up and sit with him.

Narr. 2: The eunuch was reading this passage of Scripture: "He was led like a sheep to the slaughter, and as a lamb before the shearer is silent, so he did not open his mouth. In his humiliation he was deprived of justice. Who can speak of his descendants? For his life was taken from the earth."

Solo 2: The eunuch asked Philip, "Tell me, please, who is the prophet talking about, himself or someone else?"

Narr. 1: Then Philip began with that very passage of Scripture and told him the good news about Jesus.

Narr. 2: As they traveled along the road, they came to some water and the eunuch said, "Look, here is water. Why shouldn't I be baptized?" And he gave orders to stop the chariot.

Narr. 1: Then both Philip and the eunuch went down into the water and Philip baptized him.

Narr. 2: When they came up out of the water, the Spirit of the Lord suddenly took Philip away, and the eunuch did not see him again, but went on his way rejoicing.

Acts 8:26-39

The Word in Worship:

Reaffirming the Faith

The Mercy of God

LEADER: Come, let us go up to the mountain of the Lord.

PEOPLE: Holy is his name.

SOLO 1: He will teach us his ways.

SOLO 2: Let us walk in his paths.

SOLO 3: My soul glorifies the Lord and my spirit rejoices in God my Savior, for he has been mindful of the humble state of his servant.

PEOPLE: Holy is his name.

SOLO 3: From now on all generations will call me blessed, for the Mighty One has done great things for me.

PEOPLE: Let us walk in his paths.

LEADER: A shoot will come up from the stump of Jesse,

CHOIR: A Branch which will bear fruit.

SOLO 1: The Spirit of the Lord will rest on him—

SOLO 2: The Spirit of wisdom and of understanding,

SOLO 1: The Spirit of counsel and of power,

SOLO 2: The Spirit of knowledge and of the fear of the Lord—

CHOIR: He will delight in the fear of the Lord.

SOLO 3: The mercy of God extends to those who fear him, from generation to generation.

LEADER: The law will go out from Zion,

CHOIR: The word of the Lord from Jerusalem.

SOLO 1: He will not judge by what he sees with his eyes.

SOLO 2: He will not decide by what he hears with his ears.

CHOIR: With righteousness he will judge the needy.

LEADER: With justice he will give decisions for the poor of the earth.

SOLO 3: God has performed mighty deeds with his arm.

SOLO 1: He will strike the earth with the rod of his mouth.

SOLO 2: With the breath of his lips he will slay the wicked.

CHOIR: He will crush the oppressor.

SOLO 3: God has scattered those who are proud in their inmost thoughts.

SOLO 1: He will judge between the nations.

SOLO 2: Let us beat our swords into plowshares.

Solo 1: He will settle disputes for many peoples.

Solo 2: Let us beat our spears into pruning hooks.

Leader: They will neither harm nor destroy on the holy mountain, for the earth will be full of the knowledge of the Lord as the waters cover the sea.

Solo 3: He has brought down rulers from their thrones but has lifted up the humble.

Solo 1: Nation will not take up sword against nation.

Solo 2: They will not train for war anymore.

Leader: The wolf will live with the lamb.

People: A little child will lead them.

Leader: The leopard will lie down with the goat.

People: A little child will lead them.

Leader: The calf and the lion and the yearling will lie down together.

People: A little child will lead them.

Solo 1: Righteousness will be his belt.

Solo 2: Faithfulness will be the sash around his waist.

Choir: His place of rest will be glorious.

Solo 3: God has filled the hungry with good things but has sent the rich away empty.

Leader: In that day the Root of Jesse will stand as a banner for the peoples.

Choir: The nations will rally to him.

Solo 1: He will judge your people in righteousness.

Solo 2: The mountains will bring prosperity to the people.

Solo 1: He will judge your afflicted ones with justice.

Solo 2: The hills will bring the fruit of righteousness.

Leader: He will defend the afflicted.

People: He will save the children of the needy.

Solo 1: He will endure as long as the sun.

Solo 2: He will endure as long as the moon.

People: He will endure through all generations.

Solo 1: He will be like rain falling on a mown field.

Solo 2: He will be like showers watering the earth.

People: He will rule from sea to sea.

Isaiah 2:3-5; Luke 1:46-53; Isaiah 11:1-10; Psalm 72:1-8

All We like Sheep

Leader: See, my servant will act wisely; he will be raised and lifted up.

People: He will be highly exalted.

Leader: Just as there were many who were appalled at him—

People: His appearance was so disfigured—

Leader: Just as his form was marred beyond human likeness—

People: Beyond that of any man—

Leader: So will he sprinkle many nations, and kings will shut their mouths because of him.

People: For what they were not told, they will see.

Leader: Who has believed our message and to whom has the arm of the Lord been revealed?

People: What they have not heard, they will understand.

Leader: He grew up before him like a tender shoot,

People: Like a root out of dry ground.

Leader: He had no beauty or majesty to attract us to him,

People: Nothing in his appearance that we should desire him.

Leader: He was despised and rejected by men,

People: A man of sorrows, and familiar with suffering.

Leader: Like one from whom men hide their faces he was despised.

People: We esteemed him not.

Leader: Surely he took up our infirmities and carried our sorrows, yet we considered him stricken by God,

People: Smitten by him, and afflicted.

Leader: But he was pierced for our transgressions,

People: He was crushed for our iniquities;

Leader: The punishment that brought us peace was upon him,

People: And by his wounds we are healed.

Solo 1: He was oppressed and afflicted,

Solo 2: Yet he did not open his mouth;

Solo 1: He was led like a lamb to the slaughter, and as a sheep before her shearers is silent,

Solo 2: So he did not open his mouth.

Leader: We all, like sheep, have gone astray,

People: We all, like sheep, have gone astray,

Leader: Each of us has turned to his own way;

People: Each of us has turned to his own way;

Leader: And the Lord has laid on him the iniquity of us all.

Solo 1: By oppression and judgment he was taken away.

Solo 2: And who can speak of his descendants?

Solo 1: For he was cut off from the land of the living;

Solo 2: For the transgression of my people he was stricken.

Leader: We all, like sheep, have gone astray,

People: We all, like sheep, have gone astray,

Leader: Each of us has turned to his own way;

People: Each of us has turned to his own way;

Leader: And the Lord has laid on him the iniquity of us all.

Solo 1: He was assigned a grave with the wicked, and with the rich in his death, though he had done no violence, nor was any deceit in his mouth.

Solo 2: Yet it was the Lord's will to crush him and cause him to suffer,

Solo 1: And though the Lord makes his life a guilt offering, he will see his offspring and prolong his days, and the will of the Lord will prosper in his hand.

Solo 2: After the suffering of his soul, he will see the light of life and be satisfied;

Leader: By his knowledge my righteous servant will justify many,

People: And he will bear their iniquities.

Leader: Therefore I will give him a portion among the great, and he will divide the spoils with the strong, because he poured out his life unto death,

People: And was numbered with the transgressors.

Leader: For he bore the sin of many,

People: And made intercession for the transgressors.

Leader: We all, like sheep, have gone astray, each of us has turned to his own way;

People: And the Lord has laid on him the iniquity of us all.

Isaiah 52:13—53:12

All Have Sinned

LEADER: So God created man in his own image,

MEN: In the image of God he created him;

WOMEN: Male and female he created them.

LEADER: God blessed them and said to them,

MEN: Be fruitful and multiply;

WOMEN: Fill the earth and subdue it.

MEN: Rule over the fish of the sea and the birds of the air

WOMEN: And over every living creature that moves on the ground.

LEADER: God saw all that he had made, and it was very good. And God placed the man and his wife in the Garden of Eden to work it and take care of it.

PEOPLE: The man and his wife were both naked, and they felt no shame.

LEADER: You are free to eat from any tree in the garden;

SOLO 1: But we must not eat from the tree of the knowledge of good and evil,

SOLO 2: For when we eat from it we shall surely die.

SOLO 1: Did God really say, "You must not eat from any tree in the garden?"

LEADER: Now the serpent was crafty . . .

SOLO 2: We may eat fruit from the trees in the garden,

PEOPLE: But not the tree in the middle of the garden.

SOLO 2: We must not eat from it or touch it, or we will die.

SOLO 1: You will not surely die.

LEADER: Now the serpent was crafty . . .

SOLO 1: For God knows that when you eat of it your eyes will be opened, and you will be like God, knowing good and evil.

LEADER: The woman saw that the fruit of the tree was good for food and pleasing to the eye, and also desirable for gaining wisdom;

WOMEN: She took some and ate it.

LEADER: She gave some to her husband,

WOMEN: Who was with her,

MEN: And he ate it.

LEADER: Then the eyes of both of them were opened,

PEOPLE: And they realized they were naked.

LEADER: They hid from God. And when God saw what they had done, God said to the woman,

MEN: With pain you will give birth to children.

LEADER: And to the man God said,

WOMEN: By the sweat of your brow you will eat your food.

PEOPLE: Dust we are and to dust we will return.

LEADER: Each of us has turned to our own way.

PEOPLE: We all, like sheep, have gone astray.

LEADER: All have fallen short of the glory of God.

PEOPLE: All have sinned.

GENESIS 1:27-28, 31; 2:15-17, 25; 3:1-8, 16-19; ISAIAH 53:6; ROMANS 3:23

The Kingship of Christ

LEADER: Next Sunday begins Advent. Before we start our observation of Christ's first coming, the Christian calendar provides this special day that reminds us that Christ is King. Regardless of the seeming takeover by all that's ungodly—Christ is King.

ALL: And he is our King!

LEADER: Paul, an apostle of Christ Jesus by the will of God.

MEN: To the holy and faithful brothers in Christ at Colosse:

WOMEN: Grace and peace to you from God our Father.

ALL: Who gave us Christ our King!

LEADER: Dear friends, we always thank God, the Father of our Lord Jesus Christ, when we pray for you,

CHOIR: Because we have heard of your faith in Christ Jesus and the love you have for all the saints—

WOMEN: The faith and love that spring from the hope that is stored up for you in heaven,

MEN: And that you have already heard about in the word of truth,

CHOIR: The gospel that has come to you.

ALL: Through Jesus Christ our King!

LEADER: For he has rescued us from the dominion of darkness and brought us into the kingdom of the Son he loves,

MEN: In whom we have redemption,

WOMEN: The forgiveness of sins.

ALL: Thanks be to Christ our King!

LEADER: Jesus Christ is the image of the invisible God,

CHOIR: The firstborn over all creation.

LEADER: By him all things were created:

MEN: Things in heaven,

WOMEN: And on earth,

MEN: Visible and invisible,

WOMEN: Whether thrones or powers,

MEN: Or rulers or authorities;

LEADER: All things were created by him and for him.

ALL: This is Christ our King!

LEADER: He is the head of the body, the church; he is the beginning and the firstborn from among the dead,

CHOIR: So that in everything he might have the supremacy.

LEADER: For God was pleased to have all his fullness dwell in him,

MEN: And through him to reconcile to himself all things,

WOMEN: Whether things on earth or things in heaven,

MEN: By making peace through his blood, shed on the cross.

ALL: Thanks be to Christ our King!

LEADER: Once you were alienated from God

CHOIR: And were enemies in your minds because of your evil behavior.

LEADER: But now he has reconciled you by Christ's physical body

CHOIR: Through death

LEADER: To present you holy in his sight,

WOMEN: Without blemish

MEN: And free from accusation.

LEADER: This is the gospel that you hear.

ALL: The gospel of Christ the King.

COLOSSIANS 1:1-6, 13-16, 18-23

The Word Made Flesh

SOLO 1: In the beginning was the Word,

SOLO 2: And the Word was with God,

PEOPLE: And the Word was God.

SOLO 2: He was with God in the beginning.

SOLO 1: Through him all things were made;

SOLO 2: Without him nothing was made that has been made.

SOLO 1: In him was life, and that life was the light of men.

SOLO 2: The light shines in the darkness, but the darkness has not understood it.

SOLO 3: There came a man who was sent from God; his name was John.

SOLO 4: He came as a witness to testify concerning that light, so that through him all men might believe.

SOLO 3: He himself was not the light; he came only as a witness to the light.

SOLO 1: The true light that gives light to every man was coming into the world.

SOLO 2: He was in the world, and though the world was made through him, the world did not recognize him.

Solo 3: He came to that which was his own, but his own did not receive him.

Solo 4: Yet to all who received him, to those who believed in his name, he gave the right to become children of God—

Solo 3: Children born not of natural descent,

Solo 4: Nor of human decision or a husband's will,

People: But born of God.

Solo 1: The Word became flesh and made his dwelling among us.

People: We have seen his glory,

Solo 2: The glory of the One and Only, who came from the Father,

People: Full of grace and truth.

Solo 1: The people walking in darkness have seen a great light;

Solo 2: On those living in the land of the shadow of death a light has dawned.

Right: For to us a child is born,

Left: To us a son is given,

Solo 2: And the government will be on his shoulders.

Solo 1: And he will be called Wonderful Counselor,

Right: Mighty God,

Left: Everlasting Father,

All: Prince of Peace.

Solo 3: In the past God spoke to our forefathers through the prophets at many times and in various ways,

Solo 4: But in these last days he has spoken to us by his Son,

Solo 3: Whom he appointed heir of all things,

Solo 4: And through whom he made the universe.

Solo 1: Of the increase of his government and peace there will be no end.

Solo 2: He will reign on David's throne and over his kingdom, establishing and upholding it with justice and righteousness from that time on and forever.

People: The zeal of the Lord Almighty will accomplish this.

John 1:1-14; Isaiah 9:2, 6-7;
Hebrews 1:1-2

God's Ordinances

LEADER: The law of the Lord is perfect,

PEOPLE: Reviving the soul.

LEADER: The statutes of the Lord are trustworthy,

PEOPLE: Making the wise simple.

LEADER: The precepts of the Lord are right,

PEOPLE: Giving joy to the heart.

LEADER: The commandments of the Lord are radiant,

PEOPLE: Giving light to the eyes.

LEADER: The fear of the Lord is pure,

PEOPLE: Enduring forever.

LEADER: The ordinances of the Lord are sure

PEOPLE: And altogether righteous.

MEN: They are more precious than gold,

WOMEN: Than much pure gold.

MEN: They are sweeter than honey,

WOMEN: Than honey from the comb.

LEADER: By them is your servant warned;

PEOPLE: In keeping them there is great reward.

PSALM 19:7-11

Salvation

LEADER: Come, let us walk in the light of the Lord.

PEOPLE: The Lord Our Righteousness.

LEADER: In those days and at that time I will make a righteous Branch sprout from David's line.

PEOPLE: The Lord Our Righteousness.

SOLO 1: When Christ came into the world, he said: "Sacrifice and offering you did not desire, but a body you prepared for me; with burnt offerings and sin offerings you were not pleased."

SOLO 2: He said, "Here I am—it is written about me in the scroll—I have come to do your will, O God."

LEADER: Who may ascend the hill of the Lord?

PEOPLE: He who has clean hands and a pure heart.

LEADER: Who may stand in his holy place?

PEOPLE: He who does not swear by what is false.

LEADER: Lift up your heads, O you gates; be lifted up, you ancient doors.

People: Let the King of glory come in.

Leader: Who is this King of glory?

Right: The Lord strong and mighty.

Left: The Lord mighty in battle.

Leader: Lift up your heads, O you gates; lift them up, you ancient doors.

People: Let the King of glory come in.

Leader: Who is he, this King of glory?

Right: The Lord Almighty—

Left: He is the King of glory.

Solo 1: First Christ said, "Sacrifices and offerings, burnt offerings and sin offerings you did not desire, nor were you pleased with them."

Solo 2: Then he said, "Here I am, I have come to do your will."

Leader: And by that will, we have been made holy through the sacrifice of the body of Jesus Christ once for all.

People: He has become our salvation.

Solo 1: I will trust and not be afraid.

Solo 2: The Lord, the Lord, is my strength and my song.

People: He has become our salvation.

Leader: With joy you will draw water from the wells of salvation.

People: Give thanks to the Lord.

Leader: Make known among the nations what he has done.

People: He has done glorious things.

Leader: Let this be known to all the world.

People: Great is the Holy One of Israel.

Solo 2: He will do what is just and right in the land.

People: The Lord Our Righteousness.

Psalm 24:3-4, 7-10; Isaiah 2:5; 12:2-6; Jeremiah 33:15-16; Hebrews 10:5-10

The New Birth

Narr. 1: Now there was a man of the Pharisees named Nicodemus, a member of the Jewish ruling council.

Choir: He came to Jesus at night.

Solo 1: Rabbi, we know you are a teacher who has come from God.

Narr. 2: For no one could perform the miraculous signs you are doing if God were not with him.

Solo 1: I tell you the truth, no one can see the kingdom of God unless he is born again.

Solo 2: How can a man be born when he is old?

Solo 1: Surely he cannot enter a second time into his mother's womb to be born!

Solo 2: I tell you the truth, no one can enter the kingdom of God unless he is born of water and the Spirit.

Narr. 2: Flesh gives birth to flesh, but the Spirit gives birth to spirit.

Solo 2: You should not be surprised at my saying, "You must be born again." The wind blows wherever it pleases.

Narr. 2: You hear its sound, but you cannot tell where it comes from or where it is going.

Solo 2: So it is with everyone born of the Spirit.

Solo 1: How can this be?

Solo 2: You are Israel's teacher, and do you not understand these things?

Narr. 2: I tell you the truth, we speak of what we know, and we testify to what we have seen, but still you people do not accept our testimony.

Solo 2: I have spoken to you of earthly things and you do not believe; how then will you believe if I speak of heavenly things?

Narr. 1: No one has ever gone into heaven except the one who came from heaven—the Son of Man.

Narr. 2: Just as Moses lifted up the snake in the desert, so the Son of Man must be lifted up, that everyone who believes in him may have eternal life.

Narr. 1: For God so loved the world that he gave his one and only Son, that whoever believes in him shall not perish but have eternal life.

Narr. 2: For God did not send his Son into the world to condemn the world, but to save the world through him.

John 3:1-17

Security in Christ

Leader: Be strong in the Lord and in his mighty power.

People: In Christ we are strong!

Leader: Put on the full armor of God so that you can take your stand against the devil's schemes.

People: In Christ we can stand!

Leader: Our struggle is not against flesh and blood, but against the spiritual forces of evil.

People: In Christ we are secure!

Ephesians 6:10-12

The Beatitudes

Leader: Jesus went up on a mountainside and began to teach, saying: "Blessed are the poor in spirit,

People: For theirs is the kingdom of heaven."

Leader: Jesus has also said . . .

Choir Women: Come, you who are blessed by my Father;

Choir Men: Take your inheritance, the kingdom prepared for you—

All: Prepared since the creation of the world.

Leader: Blessed are those who mourn,

People: For they will be comforted.

Leader: John in Revelation writes . . .

All: God will wipe away every tear from their eyes.

Leader: Blessed are the meek,

People: For they will inherit the earth.

Leader: From the Psalmist we read . . .

All: The meek will inherit the land and enjoy great peace.

Leader: Blessed are those who hunger and thirst for righteousness,

People: For they will be filled.

Leader: According to Isaiah . . .

Choir Women: Come, all you who are thirsty,

Choir Men: And you who have no money,

All: Come, buy and eat!

Leader: Blessed are the merciful,

People: For they will be shown mercy.

Leader: James writes . . .

All: Judgment without mercy will be shown to anyone who has not been merciful.

Leader: Blessed are the pure in heart,

People: For they shall see God.

Leader: The Psalmist asks . . .

Choir Men: Who may ascend the hill of the Lord?

Choir Women: Who may stand in his holy place?

All: He who has clean hands and a pure heart.

Leader: Blessed are the peacemakers,

People: For they shall be called sons of God.

Leader: It is James who says . . .

All: Peacemakers who sow in peace raise a harvest of righteousness.

Leader: Blessed are those who are persecuted because of righteousness.

People: For theirs is the kingdom of heaven.

Leader: Hear the words of the apostle Peter:

Choir: If you should suffer for what is right, you are blessed.

Choir Men: Do not fear what they fear;

Choir Women: Do not be frightened.

All: But in your hearts set apart Christ as Lord.

Matthew 5:1-10; 25:34; Revelation 7:17; Psalm 37:11; Isaiah 55:1; James 2:13; Psalm 24:3-4; James 3:18; 1 Peter 3:14-15

The Message of the Cross

Leader: For the message of the cross is foolishness to those who are perishing,

People: But to us who are being saved it is the power of God.

Leader: For it is written: "I will destroy the wisdom of the wise; the intelligence of the intelligent I will frustrate."

Solo 1: Where is the wise man?

Solo 2: Where is the scholar?

Solo 1: Where is the philosopher of this age?

People: Has not God made foolish the wisdom of the world?

Leader: For since in the wisdom of God the world through its wisdom did not know him, God was pleased through the foolishness of what was preached to save those who believe.

Solo 1: Jews demand miraculous signs—

People: A stumbling block to Jews.

Solo 2: Greeks look for wisdom—

People: Foolishness to Gentiles.

LEADER: But to those whom God has called, both Jews and Greeks,

PEOPLE: Christ the power of God and the wisdom of God.

LEADER: For the foolishness of God is wiser than man's wisdom, and the weakness of God is stronger than man's strength.

CHOIR: Brothers, think of what you were when you were called.

SOLO 1: Not many of you were wise by human standards;

SOLO 2: Not many were influential;

SOLO 1: Not many were of noble birth.

LEADER: But God chose the foolish things of the world to shame the wise;

PEOPLE: God chose the weak things of the world to shame the strong.

LEADER: He chose the lowly things of this world and the despised things—and the things that are not—to nullify the things that are,

PEOPLE: So that no one may boast before him.

LEADER: It is because of him that you are in Christ Jesus, who has become for us wisdom from God.

PEOPLE: Our righteousness, holiness and redemption.

1 CORINTHIANS 1:18-31

Light

LEADER: Come and worship the One who is light;

PEOPLE: God is light.

LEADER: In him there is no darkness at all.

PEOPLE: If we claim to have fellowship with him and walk in darkness,

LEADER: We lie and do not live by the truth.

WOMEN: But if we walk in the light,

MEN: As he is in the light,

LEADER: We have fellowship with one another,

ALL: And the blood of Jesus Christ, his Son, purifies us from all sin.

1 JOHN 1:5-7

A Light for the Gentiles

NARR. 1: The Lord says, "I will make you a light for the Gentiles, that you may bring my salvation to the ends of the earth."

SOLO 1: This is what the Lord says—

SOLO 2: The Redeemer and Holy One of Israel—

SOLO 3: Kings will see you and rise up, princes will see and bow down, because of the Lord, who is faithful, the Holy One of Israel, who has chosen you.

SOLO 4: I, the Lord, have called you in righteousness;

SOLO 3: I will take hold of your hand.

SOLO 4: I will keep you and will make you to be a covenant for the people.

CHOIR: A light for the Gentiles—

SOLO 1: To open eyes that are blind,

SOLO 2: To release those who sit in darkness;

SOLO 1: To free captives from prison,

SOLO 2: To release those who sit in darkness.

NARR. 1: Now there were some Greeks among those who went up to worship at the Feast. They came to Philip, who was from Bethsaida in Galilee, with a request.

CHOIR: Sir, we would like to see Jesus.

NARR. 2: Philip went to tell Andrew; Andrew and Philip in turn told Jesus. Jesus replied,

SOLO 3: The hour has come for the Son of Man to be glorified.

SOLO 4: I tell you the truth, unless a kernel of wheat falls to the ground and dies, it remains only a single seed. But if it dies, it produces many seeds.

CHOIR: The man who loves his life will lose it,

SOLO 3: While the man who hates his life in this world will keep it for eternal life.

SOLO 4: Whoever serves me must follow me; and where I am, my servant also will be. My Father will honor the one who serves me.

SOLO 3: Now my heart is troubled, and what shall I say? "Father, save me from this hour"? No, it was for this very reason I came to this hour.

SOLO 4: Father, glorify your name!

CHOIR: I have glorified it, and will glorify it again.

NARR. 1: The crowd that was there and heard it said it had thundered;

NARR. 2: Others said an angel had spoken to him.

SOLO 3: This voice was for your benefit, not mine. Now is the time for judgment on this world; now the prince of this world will be driven out.

SOLO 4: But I, when I am lifted up from the earth, will draw all men to myself.

NARR. 1: He said this to show the kind of death he was going to die.

NARR. 2: We have heard from the Law that the Christ will remain forever, so how can you say, "The Son of Man must be lifted up?"

Choir: Who is this Son of Man?

Solo 3: You are going to have the light just a little while longer. Walk while you have the light, before darkness overtakes you.

Solo 4: The man who walks in the dark does not know where he is going.

Narr. 1: Put your trust in the light while you have it, so that you may become sons of light.

Narr. 2: Both high and low among men find refuge in the shadow of your wings.

Solo 1: They feast on the abundance of your house;

Solo 2: You give them drink from your river of delights.

Narr. 1: For with you is the fountain of life;

Choir: In your light we see light.

Isaiah 49:6-7; 42:6-7; John 12:20-36; Psalm 36:7-9

A Litany of Beginning

Leader: There is a time for everything, and a season for every activity under heaven:

People: Now is the time of God's favor, now is the day of salvation.

Leader: A time to plant . . .

People: And a time to uproot.

Solo 1: A farmer went out to sow his seed. As he was scattering the seed, some fell along the path . . . Some fell on rocky places . . . Other seed fell among thorns . . . Still other seed fell on good soil, where it produced a crop. [Optional testimony]

Leader: Now is the time of God's favor,

People: Now is the day of salvation.

Leader: There is a time to be born . . .

People: And a time to die.

Solo 2: I tell you the truth, no one can see the kingdom of God unless he is born again. For God so loved the world that he gave his one and only Son, that whoever believes in him shall not perish but have eternal life. [Optional testimony]

Leader: Now is the time of God's favor,

People: Now is the day of salvation.

Leader: There is a time to kill . . .

People: And a time to heal.

Solo 3: "For your sake we face death all day long; we are considered as sheep to be slaughtered." No, in all things we are more than conquerors through him who loved us. Surely the day is coming . . . But for you who revere my name, the sun of righteousness will rise with healing in its wings. And you will go out and leap. [Optional testimony]

Leader: Now is the time of God's favor,

People: Now is the day of salvation.

Leader: There is a time to be silent . . .

People: And a time to speak.

Solo 4: Then Jesus came and said, "All authority in heaven and on earth has been given to me. Therefore go and make disciples of all nations, baptizing them in the name of the Father and of the Son and of the Holy Spirit, and teaching them to obey everything I have commanded you. And surely I am with you always, to the very end of the age." [Optional testimony]

Leader: There is a time for everything, and a season for every activity under heaven:

All: Now is the time of God's favor, now is the day of salvation.

Ecclesiastes 3:1-2; 2 Corinthians 6:2; Matthew 13:3-8; John 3:3, 16; Romans 8:36-37; Malachi 4:1-2; Matthew 28:18-20

Responding to God's Word

Leader: As the rain and the snow come down from heaven, and do not return to it without watering the earth and making it bud and flourish,

People: So that it yields seed for the sower and bread for the eater,

Leader: So is my word that goes out from my mouth:

Right: Seed for the sower—

Left: Bread for the eater—

Leader: My word will not return to me empty, but will accomplish what I desire and achieve the purpose for which I sent it.

Right: How may a young man keep his way pure?

Left: By living according to your word.

Leader: I seek you with all my heart; do not let me stray from your commands.

People: Your word is a lamp to my feet.

Leader: I have hidden your word in my heart that I might not sin against you.

People: Your word is a light for my path.

Leader: You will go out in joy and be led forth in peace; the mountains and hills will burst into song before you, and all the trees of the field will clap their hands.

Right: It is good to praise the Lord!

Left: It is good to make music to your name, O Most High!

Leader: Instead of the thornbush will grow the pine tree, and instead of briers the myrtle will grow.

Right: It is good to proclaim your love in the morning.

Left: It is good to proclaim your faithfulness at night.

Leader: This will be for the Lord's renown, for an everlasting sign, which will not be destroyed.

Right: You make me glad by your deeds, O Lord.

Left: I sing for joy at the works of your hands.

Leader: Praise be to you, O Lord; teach me your decrees.

People: Praise be to you, O Lord!

Isaiah 55:10-13; Psalm 119:9-12, 105; 92:1-2, 4

True Fasting

Leader: "Even now," declares the Lord, "return to me with all your heart, with fasting and weeping and mourning."

People: Why have we fasted, and you have not seen it?

Choir: Rend your heart and not your garments.

People: Why have we humbled ourselves, and you have not noticed?

Choir: On the day of your fasting, you do as you please.

Leader: Your fasting ends in quarreling and strife, and in striking each other with wicked fists.

Choir: You cannot fast as you do today and expect your voice to be heard on high.

People: We have fasted and we have humbled ourselves!

Leader: Is this the kind of fast I have chosen, only a day for a man to humble himself?

Choir: Is it only for bowing one's head like a reed and for lying on sackcloth and ashes?

Leader: Is that what you call a fast, a day acceptable to the Lord?

People: What should we do?

Leader: Is not this the kind of fasting I have chosen:

Solo 1: To loose the chains of injustice and untie the cords of the yoke,

Solo 2: To set the oppressed free and break every yoke?

Leader: Is it not to share your food with the hungry and to provide the poor wanderer with shelter—

Solo 1: When you see the naked, to clothe him,

Solo 2: And not to turn away from your own flesh and blood?

Leader: Then your light will break forth like the dawn—

People: Our healing will quickly appear.

Leader: Then your righteousness will go before you—

People: The glory of the Lord will be our rear guard.

LEADER: Then you will call, and the Lord will answer;

PEOPLE: We will trust in the Lord.

LEADER: You will cry for help, and he will say: Here am I.

PEOPLE: His righteousness endures forever.

JOEL 2:12-13; ISAIAH 58:3-9

Obedience and Disobedience

LEADER: Blessed is the man who does not walk in the counsel of the wicked or stand in the way of sinners or sit in the seat of mockers.

PEOPLE: Blessed is the man who delights in the law of the Lord.

LEADER: He is like a tree planted by streams of water, which yields its fruit in season and whose leaf does not wither.

PEOPLE: Blessed is the man who trusts in the Lord.

LEADER: He will be like a tree planted by the water that sends out its roots by the stream.

PEOPLE: Blessed are you who are poor, for yours is the kingdom of God.

LEADER: A tree which does not fear when heat comes; its leaves are always green.

PEOPLE: Blessed are you who hunger now, for you will be satisfied.

LEADER: A tree which has no worries in a year of drought and never fails to bear fruit.

PEOPLE: Blessed are you who weep now, for you will laugh.

LEADER: Blessed are you when men reject your name as evil, because of the Son of Man. For that is how their fathers treated the prophets.

PEOPLE: Blessed are you, true prophets of God.

LEADER: Not so the wicked! They are like chaff that the wind blows away.

PEOPLE: The way of the wicked will perish.

LEADER: Cursed is the one who trusts in man.

PEOPLE: Cursed is the one whose heart turns away from the Lord.

LEADER: Cursed is the one who depends on flesh for his strength.

PEOPLE: Woe to you who are rich, for you have already received your comfort.

LEADER: They will be like a bush in the wastelands; they will not see prosperity when it comes.

PEOPLE: Woe to you who are well fed now, for you will go hungry.

LEADER: They will dwell in the parched places of the desert, in a salt land where no one lives.

PEOPLE: Woe to you who laugh now, for you will mourn and weep.

LEADER: Woe to you when all men speak well of you, for that is how their fathers treated the false prophets.

PEOPLE: Woe to you, false prophets.

PSALM 1; JEREMIAH 17:5-8; LUKE 6:20-26

Love, Not Sacrifice

LEADER: Hear the word of the Lord!

PEOPLE: Let us acknowledge the Lord.

LEADER: The Lord has a charge to bring against you who live in the land.

PEOPLE: Let us press on to acknowledge the Lord.

LEADER: There is no faithfulness, no love, no acknowledgment of God in the land.

PEOPLE: Come, let us return to the Lord.

RIGHT: He has torn us to pieces but he will heal us;

LEFT: He has injured us but he will bind up our wounds.

LEADER: There is only cursing, lying and murder, stealing and adultery; they break all bounds, and bloodshed follows bloodshed.

RIGHT: After two days the Lord will revive us.

LEFT: On the third day he will restore us.

LEADER: Because of this the land mourns, and all who live in it waste away; the beasts of the field and the birds of the air and the fish of the sea are dying.

PEOPLE: As surely as the sun rises, the Lord will appear.

LEADER: Your love is like the morning mist, like the early dew that disappears.

RIGHT: Surely he will come to us like the winter rains.

LEFT: Surely he will come like the spring rains that water the earth.

LEADER: I cut you in pieces with my prophets, I killed you with the words of my mouth; my judgments flashed like lightning upon you.

PEOPLE: Come, let us acknowledge the Lord.

LEADER: The Lord desires mercy, not sacrifice!

People: Come, let us press on to acknowledge him.

Leader: Sow for yourselves righteousness, reap the fruit of unfailing love, and break up your unplowed ground.

People: Come, let us return to the Lord.

Leader: For it is time to seek the Lord, until he comes and showers righteousness upon you.

People: Come, let us seek the Lord.

Hosea 4:1-3; 6:1-6; 10:12

Social Justice

Choir: Hear the word of the Lord,

Leader: Because the Lord has a charge to bring against you who live in the land:

Man: There is no faithfulness,

Women: There is no love.

People: There is no acknowledgment of God in the land.

Choir: You trample on the poor and force him to give you grain.

Leader: Though you have built stone mansions, you will not live in them.

Men: Though you have planted lush vineyards,

Women: You will not drink their wine.

Choir: For I know how many are your offenses

Leader: And how great your sins.

Choir: You oppress the righteous and take bribes.

People: And you deprive the poor of justice in the courts.

Leader: Seek good, not evil, that you may live.

Choir: Then the Lord God Almighty will be with you.

Men: Hate evil, love good;

Women: Maintain justice in the courts.

People: Let justice roll on like a river.

Leader: O Lord, in keeping with all your righteous acts, turn away your anger and wrath.

Choir: We do not make requests of you because we are righteous.

People: But because of your great mercy.

Women: O Lord, listen!

Men: O Lord, forgive!

People: O Lord, hear and act!

Leader: For your sake, O my God, do not delay,

All: Because your people bear your name.

Hosea 4:1; Amos 5:11-12, 14-15, 24; Daniel 9:16, 18-19

Positive Christian Living

Leader: From Paul and Timothy to all the saints in Christ Jesus.

Men: Grace and peace to you from God our Father,

Women: And the Lord Jesus Christ.

Solo 1: "Grace and peace." The two belong together like love and hope, faith and commitment, justice and freedom.

Leader: I thank my God every time I remember you. In all my prayers for all of you, I always pray with joy.

Women: With joy!

Men: With joy!

All: With inexpressible joy that is full of glory!

Solo 2: I am confident of this, that he who began a good work in you will carry it on to completion until the day of Christ Jesus.

Leader: This is my prayer: that your love may abound more and more in knowledge and in depth of insight.

Men: So that you may be able to discern what is best

Women: And you may be pure and blameless until the day of Christ.

All: Filled with the fruit of righteousness.

Solo 1: Be filled with the fruit of the Spirit.

Solo 2: Which is love, joy, peace,

Solo 1: Patience, kindness, goodness, faithfulness,

Solo 2: Gentleness and self-control.

Leader: I will continue to rejoice,

Men: Rejoice!

Women: Rejoice!

Leader: For I know that for me to live is Christ!

Solo 1: What is it to live as Christ?

Solo 2: How is it to be like Christ?

Leader: First of all, your attitude should be the same as that of Christ Jesus:

Men: Who, being in very nature God,

Women: Did not consider equality with God something to be grasped,

MEN: But made himself nothing,

WOMEN: Taking the very image of a servant,

ALL: And being made in human likeness.

SOLO 1: Human likeness.

LEADER: The Creator God said,

SOLO 2: Let us make man in our image,

SOLO 1: In our likeness.

SOLO 2: So God created man in his own image,

SOLO 1: In the image of God he created him;

SOLO 2: Male and female he created them.

ALL: Then God saw all that he had made, and it was very good.

LEADER: Christ, being found in appearance as a man, humbled himself and became obedient to death—

ALL: Even death on a cross!

SOLO 1: Jesus! Why do you hang there with nails in your hands and feet?

SOLO 2: Jesus! Why are you on that cross with a spear wound in your side?

ALL: Because I love you.

LEADER: Then God exalted him to the highest place and gave him the name that is above every name.

MEN: Wonderful Counselor,

WOMEN: Mighty God,

MEN: Everlasting Father,

ALL: Prince of Peace.

LEADER: At the name of Jesus every knee should bow,

WOMEN: In heaven

MEN: And on earth

ALL: And under the earth,

LEADER: And every tongue confess that Jesus Christ is Lord

MEN: Jesus Christ is Lord!

WOMEN: Jesus Christ is Lord!

ALL: He is Lord, to the glory of God the Father.

PHILIPPIANS 1:1-4, 6, 9-11, 18-19, 21; 2:5-11; GALATIANS 5:22-23; GENESIS 1:26-27, 31; ISAIAH 9:6

Assurance

LEADER: All of you saints who are gathered here this morning [afternoon] [evening].

PEOPLE: We, whose names are in the book of life.

LEADER: Rejoice in the Lord always.

PEOPLE: We will say it again: Rejoice!

LEADER: Let your gentleness be evident to all.

MEN: The Lord is near.

LEADER: Do not be anxious about anything.

WOMEN: Present your requests to God.

LEADER: And the peace of God will guard your hearts

MEN: And your minds in Christ Jesus.

ALL: And the God of peace will be with us.

PHILIPPIANS 4:3-7, 9

Christian Conduct

LEADER: Since you have been raised with Christ, set your hearts on things above,

PEOPLE: Where Christ is seated at the right hand of God.

MEN: We set our minds on things above,

WOMEN: Not on earthly things.

LEADER: For you died,

PEOPLE: And our lives are now hidden with Christ in God.

LEADER: When Christ, who is your life, appears, then you also will appear with him in glory.

PEOPLE: We will appear with Christ in glory.

WOMEN: With Christ . . .

MEN: In glory!

LEADER: Put to death, therefore, whatever belongs to your earthly nature:

CHOIR: Sexual immorality, impurity, lust, evil desires and greed,

PEOPLE: All of which is idolatry.

LEADER: Because of these, the wrath of God is coming.

PEOPLE: We used to walk in these ways, in the life we once lived.

LEADER: But now you must rid yourselves of all such things as these:

CHOIR: Anger, rage, malice, slander, and filthy language from your lips.

LEADER: Do not lie to each other, since you have taken off your old self with its practices,

PEOPLE: And we have put on our new self,

LEADER: Which is being renewed in knowledge in the image of its Creator.

ALL: Christ is all, and is in all.

COLOSSIANS 3:1-11

While It Is Yet Day

LEADER: Do not say, Four months more and then the harvest.

CHOIR: Open your eyes and look at the fields!

PEOPLE: They are ripe for the harvest.

LEADER: Even now the reaper draws his wages,

PEOPLE: Even now he harvests the crop for eternal life,

CHOIR: So that the sower and the reaper may be glad together.

LEADER: Thus the saying "One sows and another reaps" is true.

CHOIR: I sent you to reap what you have not worked for.

PEOPLE: Others have done the hard work, and we have reaped the benefits of their labor.

LEADER: As long as it is day, we must do the work of him who sent me.

CHOIR: Night is coming, when no one can work.

LEADER: Let us not be weary in doing good, for at the proper time we will reap a harvest.

PEOPLE: If we do not give up.

JOHN 4:35-38; 9:4; GALATIANS 6:9

The Day Is Almost Here

LEADER: The hour has come for you to wake up from your slumber,

CHOIR: Because our salvation is nearer now than when we first believed.

PEOPLE: The night is nearly over.

LEADER: So let us put aside the deeds of darkness and put on the armor of light.

PEOPLE: The day is almost here!

LEADER: No one knows about that day or hour,

RIGHT: Not even the angels in heaven,

LEFT: Nor the Son,

PEOPLE: But only the Father.

LEADER: As it was in the days of Noah, so it will be at the coming of the Son of Man.

PEOPLE: As it was in the days of Noah—

LEADER: For in the days before the flood, people were eating and drinking, marrying and giving in marriage, up to the day Noah entered the ark;

PEOPLE: As it was in the days of Noah—

LEADER: They knew nothing about what would happen until the flood came and took them all away. That is how it will be at the coming of the Son of Man.

PEOPLE: As it was in the days of Noah—

LEADER: Two men will be in the field;

PEOPLE: One will be taken and the other left.

LEADER: Two women will be grinding with a hand mill;

PEOPLE: One will be taken and the other left.

LEADER: Therefore keep watch,

CHOIR: Because you do not know on what day your Lord will come.

LEADER: Therefore you do not lack any spiritual gift as you eagerly wait for our Lord Jesus Christ to be revealed.

PEOPLE: Our salvation is nearer now—

LEADER: He will keep you strong to the end,

CHOIR: So that you will be blameless on the day of our Lord Jesus Christ.

PEOPLE: The night is nearly over.

LEADER: God, who has called you into fellowship with his Son Jesus Christ our Lord, is faithful.

PEOPLE: The day is almost here!

ROMANS 13:11-12; MATTHEW 24:36-42;
1 CORINTHIANS 1:7-9

Come, Lord Jesus!

Leader: But do not forget this one thing, dear friends:

Choir: With the Lord a day is like a thousand years,

People: And a thousand years are like a day.

Leader: The Lord is not slow in keeping his promise, as some understand slowness.

Choir: He is patient with you,

People: But the day of the Lord will come like a thief.

Choir: He does not want anyone to perish, but everyone to come to repentance.

People: But the day of the Lord will come like a thief.

Right: The heavens will disappear with a roar;

Left: The elements will be destroyed by fire,

People: And the earth and everything in it will be laid bare.

Leader: Since everything will be destroyed in this way, what kind of people ought you to be?

People: We ought to live holy and godly lives.

Leader: The day of God will bring about the destruction of the heavens by fire, and the elements will melt in the heat.

Choir: But in keeping with his promise we are looking forward to a new heaven and a new earth,

People: The home of righteousness.

Leader: So then, dear friends, since you are looking forward to this, make every effort to be found spotless, blameless and at peace with him.

Choir: Be patient, then, brothers, until the Lord's coming.

Leader: See how the farmer waits for the land to yield its valuable crop and how patient he is for the autumn and spring rains.

Right: We will be patient.

Left: We will stand firm.

People: The Lord's coming is near.

Leader: Don't grumble against each other, brothers, or you will be judged.

People: The Judge is standing at the door!

Leader: May your whole spirit, soul and body be kept blameless at the coming of our Lord Jesus Christ.

People: Maranatha!

Leader: The one who calls you is faithful and he will do it.

People: Come, Lord Jesus!

2 Peter 3:8-14; James 5:7-9;
1 Thessalonians 5:23-24

What God Has Joined

LEADER: God created man in his own image,

MEN: In the image of God he created them;

WOMEN: Male and female he created them.

LEADER: And a man will leave his father and his mother and be united to his wife,

PEOPLE: And they will become one flesh.

LEADER: What God has joined together, let no one separate.

MEN: Bone of my bone.

WOMEN: Flesh of my flesh.

MEN: Place me like a seal over your heart,

WOMEN: Like a seal upon your arm.

LEADER: What God has joined together,

PEOPLE: Let no one separate.

LEADER: Catch for us the foxes, the little foxes, that ruin the vineyards.

WOMEN: Love is patient and kind;

MEN: Love does not envy or boast.

LEADER: The little foxes . . .

WOMEN: Love is not proud or rude.

MEN: Love is not self-seeking or easily angered.

PEOPLE: The little foxes . . .

MEN: Love keeps no record of wrongs.

WOMEN: Love does not delight in evil but rejoices with the truth.

PEOPLE: The little foxes that ruin the vineyards.

MEN: Love always protects, always trusts;

WOMEN: Love always hopes, always perseveres.

PEOPLE: Love never fails.

WOMEN: For love is as strong as death,

MEN: Passion fierce as the grave.

WOMEN: Love burns like blazing fire,

MEN: Like a mighty flame.

WOMEN: Many waters cannot quench love;

MEN: Rivers cannot wash it away.

LEADER: If one were to give all the wealth of his house for love, it would be utterly scorned.

PEOPLE: Love never fails.

GENESIS 1:27; 2:23-24; SONG OF SONGS 2:15; 8:6-7; MATTHEW 19:6; 1 CORINTHIANS 13:4-8

A Wedding Ceremony Reading

Leader: Before these your family and friends, let me remind you, *[Woman]* and *[Man]*, that love is kind . . . never jealous . . . never prideful . . . never selfish. Love does not demand its own way.

People: Love is big enough to share . . . to give . . . to spend . . . to release . . . to allow . . . to build up . . . to understand . . . to thoroughly enjoy.

Leader: If you love someone, you will trust in him or her. You will always expect the best.

People: How great is the love the Father has lavished on us, that we should be called children of God!

Women: This is the message you heard from the beginning: We should love one another.

Men: Let us not love with words or tongue but with actions and in truth.

Leader: *[Man]*, place *[Woman]* like a seal over your heart, like a seal on your arm.

People: For love is as strong as death.

Leader: It burns like blazing fire,

People: Like a mighty flame.

Leader: Many waters cannot quench love;

People: Rivers cannot wash it away.

Leader: If one were to give all the wealth of his house for love, it would be utterly scorned.

People: In *[Man]* and *[Woman]* abide faith, hope and love. But the greatest of these is love.

Based on 1 Corinthians 13; 1 John 3:1, 11, 18; Song of Songs 8:6-7

For Christian Parents

LEADER: O my people, hear my teaching;

PEOPLE: Listen to the words of my mouth.

LEADER: I will open my mouth in parables.

PEOPLE: I will utter hidden things, things from old—

LEADER: Things we have heard and known,

PEOPLE: Things our fathers have told us.

LEADER: We will not hide them from our children;

PEOPLE: We will tell the next generation the praiseworthy deeds of the Lord.

PSALM 78:1-4

Members Together of One Body

SOLO 1: Surely you have heard about the administration of God's grace, that is, the mystery made known by revelation—

SOLO 2: This mystery is that through the gospel the Gentiles are heirs together with Israel,

SOLO 1: Members together of one body,

SOLO 2: Sharers together in the promise in Christ Jesus.

SOLO 1: God's intent was that now, through the church, the manifold wisdom of God should be made known to the rulers and authorities in the heavenly realms.

SOLO 2: According to his eternal purpose which he accomplished in Christ Jesus our Lord.

SOLO 1: In him we may approach God with freedom.

SOLO 2: Through faith in him we may approach God with confidence.

EPHESIANS 3:2-12

The Word in Worship:

Reflecting the Faith

The Earth Is the Lord's

LEADER: The earth is the Lord's, and everything in it,

CHOIR: The world, and all who live in it;

LEADER: For he founded it upon the seas

PEOPLE: And established it upon the waters.

LEADER: Who may ascend the hill of the Lord? Who may stand in his holy place?

CHOIR: He who has clean hands and a pure heart,

MEN: Who does not lift up his soul to an idol

WOMEN: Or swear by what is false.

PEOPLE: He will receive blessing from the Lord and vindication from God his Savior.

LEADER: Such is the generation of those who seek him,

CHOIR: Who seek your face, O God of Jacob.

ALL: Selah.

LEADER: Lift up your heads, O ye gates;

PEOPLE: Be lifted up, you ancient doors,

CHOIR: So the King of glory may come in.

LEADER: Who is this King of glory?

PEOPLE: The Lord strong and mighty,

CHOIR: The Lord mighty in battle.

LEADER: Lift up your heads, O ye gates;

PEOPLE: Lift them up, you ancient doors,

CHOIR: That the King of glory may come in.

LEADER: Who is he, this King of glory?

PEOPLE: The Lord Almighty—

ALL: He is the King of glory.

PSALM 24

The Good Things of God

LEADER: Praise awaits you, O God, in Zion; to you our vows will be fulfilled.

PEOPLE: O you who hear prayer, to you all men will come.

LEADER: When we were overwhelmed by sins, you forgave our transgressions.

PEOPLE: Blessed are those you choose and bring near to live in your courts!

LEADER: We are filled with the good things of your house.

PEOPLE: We are filled with the good things of your holy temple.

LEADER: You answer us with awesome deeds of righteousness, O God our Savior, the hope of all the ends of the earth and of the farthest seas.

PEOPLE: Those living far away fear your wonders.

LEADER: Our God who formed the mountains by your power, having armed yourself with strength, who stilled the roaring of the seas, the roaring of their waves, and the turmoil of the nations.

PEOPLE: Where morning dawns and evening fades you call forth songs of joy.

LEADER: The streams of God are filled with water to provide the people with grain,

PEOPLE: For so you have ordained it.

LEADER: You care for the land and water it.

PEOPLE: You enrich it abundantly.

LEADER: You drench its furrows and level its ridges; you soften it with showers and bless its crops.

PEOPLE: You crown the year with your bounty.

LEADER: The grasslands of the desert overflow; the hills are clothed with gladness.

PEOPLE: Your carts overflow with abundance.

LEADER: The meadows are covered with flocks and the valleys are mantled with grain;

PEOPLE: They shout for joy and sing!

LEADER: Praise awaits you, O God, in Zion; to you our vows will be fulfilled.

PEOPLE: O you who hear prayer, to you all men will come.

LEADER: When we were overwhelmed by sins, you forgave our transgressions.

PEOPLE: Blessed are those you choose and bring near to live in your courts!

PSALM 65

Gratitude

Leader: In praise of God's mercy!

People: I love the Lord,

Women: For he heard my voice;

Men: He heard my cry for mercy.

People: Because he turned his ear to me,

Men: I will call on him as long as I live.

Leader: In praise of God's care!

People: The cords of death entangled me,

Men: The anguish of the grave came upon me;

People: I was overcome by trouble and sorrow.

Women: Then I called on the name of the Lord:

People: "O Lord, save me!"

Leader: In praise of God's concern!

People: The Lord is gracious and righteous;

Women: Our God is full of compassion.

People: The Lord protects the simple-hearted;

Men: When I was in great need, he saved me.

Leader: In praise of God's goodness!

People: Be at rest once more, O my soul, for the Lord has been good to me.

Leader: In praise of God's strength!

Men: For you, O Lord, have delivered my soul from death,

Women: My eyes from tears,

Men: My feet from stumbling,

People: That I may walk before the Lord in the land of the living.

Leader: In praise of God's goodness!

People: How can I repay the Lord for all his goodness to me?

Men: I will lift up the cup of salvation.

Women: I will call on the name of the Lord.

People: I will fulfill my vows to the Lord in the presence of all his people.

Leader: In praise of God's presence!

Women: I will sacrifice a thank offering to you.

People: I will call on the name of the Lord.

Men: I will fulfill my vows to the Lord in the presence of all his people,

People: In the courts of the house of the Lord—

Women: I will fulfill my vows in your midst.

People: Praise the Lord.

Psalm 116:1-9, 12-14, 17-19

He Who Comes in the Name of the Lord

SOLO 1: Open for me the gates of righteousness; I will enter and give thanks to the Lord.

LEADER: This is the gate of the Lord through which the righteous may enter.

SOLO 1: I will give you thanks, for you answered me; you have become my salvation.

LEADER: The stone the builders rejected has become the capstone;

CHOIR: The Lord has done this.

PEOPLE: It is marvelous in our eyes.

LEADER: This is the day the Lord has made.

PEOPLE: Let us rejoice and be glad in it.

LEADER: Blessed is he who comes in the name of the Lord.

PEOPLE: From the house of the Lord we bless you.

LEADER: The Lord is God,

PEOPLE: He has made his light shine upon us.

NARR. 1: As they approached Jerusalem and came to Bethphage on the Mount of Olives, Jesus sent two disciples, saying to them,

SOLO 1: Go to the village ahead of you, and at once you will find a donkey tied there, with her colt by her. Untie them and bring them to me. If anyone says anything to you, tell him that the Lord needs them, and he will send them right away.

NARR. 1: This took place to fulfill what was spoken through the prophet:

NARR. 2: Say to the Daughter of Zion, "See, your king comes to you, gentle and riding on a donkey, on a colt, the foal of a donkey."

NARR. 1: The disciples went and did as Jesus had instructed them.

NARR. 2: They brought the donkey and the colt, placed their cloaks on them, and Jesus sat on them.

NARR. 1: A very large crowd spread their cloaks on the road, while others cut branches from the trees and spread them on the road.

NARR. 2: The crowds that went ahead of him and those that followed shouted,

PEOPLE: Hosanna to the Son of David!

CHOIR: Blessed is he who comes in the name of the Lord!

PEOPLE: Hosanna in the highest!

NARR. 1: When Jesus entered Jerusalem, the whole city was stirred and asked, "Who is this?"

NARR. 2: The crowds answered, "This is Jesus, the prophet from Nazareth in Galilee."

LEADER: With boughs in hand, join in the festal procession up to the horns of the altar.

CHOIR: You are my God, and I will give you thanks.

PEOPLE: You are my God, and I will exalt you.

LEADER: Give thanks to the Lord, for he is good.

PEOPLE: His love endures forever.

LEADER: This is the day the Lord has made.

PEOPLE: Let us rejoice and be glad in it.

LEADER: Blessed is he who comes in the name of the Lord.

PEOPLE: From the house of the Lord we bless you.

LEADER: Who is this who comes in the name of the Lord?

PEOPLE: Jesus!

PSALM 118:19-29; MATTHEW 21:1-11

Joy in the Lord

LEADER: Come, let us rejoice in him.

RIGHT: The Lord has done great things for us.

LEFT: We are filled with joy.

LEADER: When the Lord brought back the captives to Zion, they were like men who dreamed.

PEOPLE: The Lord had done great things for them.

SOLO 1: Their mouths were filled with laughter.

SOLO 2: Their tongues were filled with songs of joy.

PEOPLE: They were filled with joy.

SOLO 1: Do not fear, O Zion.

SOLO 2: The Lord your God is with you.

PEOPLE: He is mighty to save.

SOLO 1: The desert and the parched land will be glad.

SOLO 2: The wilderness will rejoice and blossom.

SOLO 1: The wilderness will burst into bloom like the crocus.

SOLO 2: The wilderness will rejoice greatly and shout for joy.

PEOPLE: They will see the glory of the Lord.

SOLO 1: Strengthen the feeble hands.

SOLO 2: Be strong, do not fear.

SOLO 1: Steady the knees that give way.

SOLO 2: Be strong, do not fear.

PEOPLE: Your God will come.

SOLO 1: The eyes of the blind will be opened.

SOLO 2: The ears of the deaf will be unstopped.

SOLO 1: The lame will leap like a deer.

SOLO 2: The mute tongue will shout for joy.

PEOPLE: Come, Lord Jesus.

LEADER: Those who sow in tears will reap with songs of joy.

People: The Lord has done great things for us.

Leader: Those who go out weeping will return with songs of joy.

People: We are filled with joy.

Psalm 126:1-6; Zephaniah 3:16-17; Isaiah 35:1-6

Marks of a Christian

Leader: These are the words of the apostle Paul, a Christian brother:

People: I always thank my God as I remember you in my prayers,

Leader: Because I hear about your faith in the Lord Jesus,

People: And your love for all the saints.

Leader: I pray that you may be active in sharing your faith, so that you will have a full understanding of every good thing we have in Christ.

People: God grant that for us too.

Philemon 4-6

To Heal the Suffering

Leader: How good it is to sing praises to our God, how pleasant and fitting to praise him!

People: Great is our Lord!

Solo 1: Does not man have hard service on earth?

Solo 2: Are not his days like those of a hired man?

Solo 1: We are like a slave longing for the evening shadows.

Solo 2: We are like a hired man waiting eagerly for his wages.

Leader: The Lord heals the brokenhearted and binds up their wounds.

People: The Lord is mighty in power.

Solo 1: I have been allotted months of futility. Nights of misery have been assigned to me.

Solo 2: When I lie down I think, "How long before I get up?" The night drags on, and I toss till dawn.

Leader: The Lord determines the number of the stars and calls them each by name.

People: His understanding has no limit.

Solo 1: My body is clothed with worms and scabs, my skin is broken and festering.

Solo 2: My days are swifter than a weaver's shuttle, and they come to an end without hope.

Leader: The Lord sustains the humble but casts the wicked to the ground.

People: Sing to the Lord with thanksgiving.

Leader: He covers the sky with clouds; he supplies the earth with rain and makes grass grow on the hills. He provides food for the cattle and for the young ravens when they call.

People: Make music to our God on the harp.

Solo 1: Remember, O God, that my life is but a breath.

Solo 2: My eyes will never see happiness again.

Leader: His pleasure is not in the strength of the horse, nor his delight in the legs of a man; the Lord delights in those who fear him,

People: Those who put their hope in his unfailing love.

Job 7:1-7; Psalm 147:1-11

Glory Forever!

LEADER: Oh, the depth of the riches of the wisdom and knowledge of God!

PEOPLE: How unsearchable his judgments,

CHOIR: And his paths beyond tracing out!

LEADER: Who has known the mind of the Lord?

PEOPLE: Or who has been his counselor?

LEADER: Who has ever given to God,

CHOIR: That God should repay him?

LEADER: For from him and through him and to him are all things.

ALL: To him be the glory forever! Amen.

ROMANS 11:33-36

What God Has Prepared

LEADER: No eye has seen,

PEOPLE: No ear has heard,

WOMEN: No mind has conceived

MEN: What God has prepared

PEOPLE: For those who love him.

LEADER: But God has revealed it to us by his Spirit.

1 CORINTHIANS 2:9-10

The Song of Moses

LEADER: The Israelites went through the sea on dry ground,

PEOPLE: With a wall of water on their right and on their left.

LEADER: That day the Lord saved Israel from the hands of the Egyptians. And when the Israelites saw the great power the Lord displayed against the Egyptians, the people feared the Lord.

PEOPLE: And the people put their trust in the Lord and in Moses his servant.

LEADER: Then Moses and the Israelites sang this song to the Lord:

MEN: I will sing to the Lord, for he is highly exalted.

PEOPLE: The horse and its rider he has hurled into the sea.

MEN: The Lord is my strength and my song;

PEOPLE: He has become my salvation.

WOMEN: He is my God, and I will praise him,

PEOPLE: My father's God, and I will exalt him.

MEN: The Lord is a warrior;

WOMEN: The Lord is his name.

MEN: Pharaoh's chariots and his army he has hurled into the sea.

PEOPLE: The best of Pharaoh's officers are drowned in the Red Sea.

LEADER: The deep waters have covered them; they sank to the depths like a stone.

MEN: Your right hand, O Lord, was majestic in power.

WOMEN: Your right hand, O Lord, shattered the enemy.

PEOPLE: In the greatness of your majesty you threw down those who opposed you.

LEADER: Who among the gods is like you, O Lord?

PEOPLE: Who is like you—

WOMEN: Majestic in holiness,

MEN: Awesome in glory,

WOMEN: Working wonders?

LEADER: In your unfailing love you will lead the people you have redeemed.

ALL: In your strength you will guide them to your holy dwelling.

LEADER: You will bring them in and plant them on the mountain of your inheritance—

People: The place, O Lord, you made for your dwelling,

Leader: The sanctuary, O Lord, your hands have established.

All: The Lord will reign for ever and ever.

Exodus 14:29-31; 15:1-7, 11, 13, 17-18

God's Provisions

Leader: Observe the commands of the Lord your God,

People: Walking in his ways and revering him.

Women: For the Lord your God is bringing you into a good land—

Men: A land with streams and pools of water,

People: With springs flowing in the valleys and hills;

Leader: A land with wheat and barley, vines and fig trees, pomegranates, olive oil and honey.

People: A land where bread will not be scarce and you will lack nothing.

Leader: When you have eaten and are satisfied, praise the Lord your God.

People: Be careful that you do not forget the Lord your God.

Women: When you eat and are satisfied,

Men: When you build fine houses and settle down,

Women: When your herds and flocks grow large

Men: And your silver and gold increase,

People: And all you have is multiplied,

Leader: Remember the Lord your God, for it is he who gives you the ability to produce wealth,

People: And so confirms his covenant, which he swore to your forefathers, as it is today.

Deuteronomy 8:6-13, 18

God's Justice

DAVID: O Lord my God . . . O Lord . . . O Lord, my God; my protection . . . my shepherd. Give me words to celebrate your justice . . . your fairness . . . your protection in time of trouble. I remember well as a lad, when a fierce lion came to attack and kill, my father's sheep were his prey; you, O Lord my God, were with me.

LEADER: O Lord my God,

PEOPLE: I take refuge in you;

MEN: Save and deliver me from all who pursue me. Or they will tear me like a lion

WOMEN: And rip me to pieces with no one to rescue me.

LEADER: O Lord my God,

PEOPLE: If I have done this and there is guilt on my hands—

MEN: If I have done evil to him who is at peace with me or without cause have robbed my foe—

WOMEN: Then let my enemy pursue and overtake me;

MEN: Let him trample my life to the ground and make me sleep in the dust.

PEOPLE: Selah.

DAVID: I appeal to your court of justice, O Lord. My enemies are near. They stand at ready to attack from every side. You are just and love mercy. I am innocent and plead for your justice.

LEADER: Arise, O Lord, arise in your anger.

PEOPLE: Rise up against the rage of my enemies.

WOMEN: Awake, my God;

MEN: Decree justice.

WOMEN: Let the assembled peoples gather around you.

PEOPLE: Rule over them from on high;

MEN: Judge me, O Lord, according to my righteousness,

PEOPLE: According to my integrity, O Most High.

DAVID: I have learned that God's righteousness is his faithfulness to his people. He is like an earthly king to whom those with no power look for protection, the oppressed for justice, and the needy for help.

LEADER: O righteous God, who searches minds and hearts,

MEN: Bring to an end the violence of the wicked

WOMEN: And make the righteous secure.

LEADER: My shield is God Most High,

PEOPLE: Who saves the upright in heart.

LEADER: God is a righteous judge,

PEOPLE: A God who expresses his wrath every day.

DAVID: God's justice is His righteousness.

LEADER: I will give thanks to the Lord

WOMEN: Because of his righteousness.

MEN: I will sing praise

PEOPLE: To the name of the Lord Most High.

PSALM 7:1-11, 17

His Promises

Leader: Let us remember Christ Jesus.

People: If we die with him,

Leader: We will also live with him;

People: If we endure,

Leader: We will also reign with him.

People: If we disown him,

Leader: He will also disown us;

People: If we are faithless,

Leader: He will remain faithful,

All: For he cannot disown himself.

2 Timothy 2:8, 11-13

Together with Him

Leader: We believe that Jesus died and rose again.

People: We believe that God will bring with Jesus those who have fallen asleep in him.

Leader: For the Lord himself will come down from heaven, with a loud command,

People: With the voice of the archangel and with the trumpet call of God.

Leader: The dead in Christ will rise first.

People: After that, we who are still alive and are left will be caught up together with them in the clouds to meet the Lord in the air.

Leader: And so we will be with the Lord forever.

People: And forever and forever. Amen.

1 Thessalonians 4:14, 16-17

The New Jerusalem

Leader: The revelation of Jesus Christ, which God gave John. Blessed are those who hear this prophecy and take it to heart, because the time is near.

Solo 1: From John: grace and peace to you from him who is, and who was, and who is to come.

Solo 2: I am the Alpha and the Omega, one who is, and who was, and who is to come, the Almighty.

Choir: He who has an ear, let him hear.

Solo 1: I John saw a new heaven and a new earth,

Choir: For the first heaven and the first earth had passed away, and there was no longer any sea.

Solo 1: I saw the Holy City, the new Jerusalem, coming down out of heaven.

Choir: She was prepared as a bride beautifully dressed for her husband.

Solo 1: And I heard a loud voice from the throne,

Solo 2: Now the dwelling of God is with men, and he will live with them.

Choir: They will be his people,

Solo 2: And God himself will be with them and be their God.

Choir: He will wipe every tear from their eyes.

Solo 2: There will be no more death or mourning or crying or pain.

Solo 1: He who was seated on the throne said,

Solo 2: I am making everything new! I am the Alpha and the Omega,

Choir: The Beginning and the End.

Solo 2: To him who is thirsty I will give to drink without cost from the spring of the water of life.

Solo 1: I will be his God and he will be my son.

Solo 2: But the cowardly, the unbelieving, the vile,

Solo 1: The murderers, the sexually immoral,

Solo 2: Those who practice magic arts,

Solo 1: The idolaters and all liars—

Solo 2: Their place will be in the fiery lake of burning sulfur.

Leader: Then one of seven angels said, "Come, I will show you the bride, the wife of the Lamb."

Solo 1: And he came and carried me away in the Spirit to a mountain great and high and showed me the Holy City, Jerusalem, coming down out of heaven from God.

Solo 2: It shone with the glory of God.

Solo 1: Its brilliance was like that of a very special jewel,

Solo 2: Like a jasper,

Solo 1: Clear as crystal.

Leader: The city had a great high wall with twelve gates, and with twelve angels at the gates.

Solo 1: On the gates were written the names of the twelve tribes of Israel.

Solo 2: There were three gates on the east,

Solo 1: Three on the north,

Solo 2: Three on the south,

Solo 1: Three on the west.

Leader: The wall of the city had twelve foundations, and on them were the names of the twelve apostles of the Lamb.

Solo 1: The wall was made of jasper,

Choir: And the city of pure gold, as pure as glass.

Leader: The foundations of the city walls were decorated with every kind of precious stone.

Solo 1: The first foundation was jasper,

Solo 2: The second sapphire,

Leader: The third chalcedony,

Solo 1: The fourth emerald,

Solo 2: The fifth sardonyx,

Choir: The sixth carnelian,

Solo 1: The seventh chrysolite,

Solo 2: The eighth beryl,

Leader: The ninth topaz,

Solo 1: The tenth chrysoprase,

Solo 2: The eleventh jacinth,

Choir: The twelfth amethyst.

Leader: The twelve gates were twelve pearls, each gate made of a single pearl. The great street of the city . . .

Choir: Was of pure gold.

Leader: Like transparent glass.

Solo 1: I did not see a temple in the city,

Solo 2: Because the Lord God Almighty and the Lamb are its temple.

Leader: The city does not need the sun or the moon to shine on it,

Choir: For the glory of God gives it light.

Leader: And the Lamb is its lamp.

Solo 1: The nations will walk by its light,

Solo 2: And the kings of the earth will bring their splendor into it.

Solo 1: On no day will its gates ever be shut.

Choir: For there will be no night there.

Leader: The glory and honor of the nations will be brought into it.

Solo 2: Nothing impure will ever enter it,

Solo 1: Nor will anyone who does what is shameful or deceitful,

Choir: But only those whose names are written in the Lamb's book of life.

Leader: The grace of the Lord Jesus be with God's people.

All: Amen.

Revelation 1:1, 3-4, 8; 2:7; 21:1-14, 18-27; 22:21

David's God: King and Shepherd

DAVID: You ask to see God; to know what he is like. I have seen him in many ways. I have seen his power unleashed like a storm and set great forces into motion.

MEN: You are mighty, O Lord, and your faithfulness surrounds you.

WOMEN: You rule over the surging sea;

CHOIR: When its waves mount up, you still them.

CHOIR MEN: The heavens are yours,

CHOIR WOMEN: And yours also the earth;

PEOPLE: You founded the world and all that is in it.

MEN: You created the north and the south;

WOMEN: Mounts Tabor and Hermon sing for joy at your name.

MEN: Your arm is endued with power;

WOMEN: Your hand is strong,

PEOPLE: Your right hand is exalted.

DAVID: What is God like? To what shall I compare him? Oh, I have seen him and I know him. To me . . .

CHOIR: The Lord is robed in majesty and armed with strength.

PEOPLE: The Lord God is a sun and shield.

WOMEN: The Lord bestows favor and honor.

PEOPLE: No good thing does he withhold for those whose walk is blameless.

DAVID: The God I served as a boy was the sheepherder's God. Today, he is still the loving One who is called the Good Shepherd.

PEOPLE: The Lord is my shepherd, I shall not be in want.

MEN: He makes me lie down in green pastures,

WOMEN: He leads me beside quiet waters,

PEOPLE: He restores my soul.

DAVID: He guides me in the paths of righteousness for his name's sake.

CHOIR: Even though I walk through the valley of the shadow of death, I will fear no evil,

PEOPLE: For you are with me.

MEN: Your rod and your staff, they comfort me.

DAVID: Our Shepherd-King receives us at his table and protects us.

PEOPLE: You prepare a table before me in the presence of my enemies.

WOMEN: You anoint my head with oil;

MEN: My cup overflows.

DAVID: Even as a young shepherd, I was aware of God's covenant, his unfailing love.

PEOPLE: Surely goodness and love will follow me all the days of my life.

DAVID: And I will dwell in the house of the Lord

ALL: Forever.

PSALM 89:8-13; 93:1; 84:11; 23

The Lord Is My Shepherd

SOLO 1: Jesus said, "I tell you the truth, I am the gate of the sheep.

SOLO 2: All who ever came before me were thieves and robbers, but the sheep did not listen to them."

LEADER: The Lord is my shepherd.

PEOPLE: I shall not be in want.

SOLO 1: Jesus said, "I am the gate; whoever enters through me will be saved.

SOLO 2: He will come in and go out, and find pasture."

LEADER: The Lord is my shepherd.

PEOPLE: He makes me lie down in green pastures.

LEADER: The Lord is my shepherd.

PEOPLE: He leads me beside quiet waters.

SOLO 1: Jesus said, "I am the good shepherd.

SOLO 2: The good shepherd lays down his life for the sheep."

LEADER: The Lord is my shepherd.

PEOPLE: He restores my soul.

LEADER: The Lord is my shepherd.

PEOPLE: He guides me in paths of righteousness for his name's sake.

SOLO 1: The hired hand is not the shepherd who owns the sheep. So when he sees the wolf coming, he abandons the sheep and runs away.

SOLO 2: Then the wolf attacks the flock and scatters it. The man runs away because he is a hired hand and cares nothing for the sheep.

LEADER: Even though I walk through the valley of the shadow of death, I will fear no evil,

PEOPLE: For you are with me;

LEADER: Your rod and your staff, they comfort me.

PEOPLE: The Lord is my shepherd.

LEADER: You prepare a table before me in the presence of my enemies.

People: The Lord is my shepherd.

Solo 1: Jesus said, "I am the good shepherd;

Solo 2: I know my sheep and my sheep know me—just as the Father knows me and I know the Father."

Leader: You anoint my head with oil;

People: My cup overflows.

Solo 1: Jesus said, "I am the good shepherd;

Solo 2: I lay down my life for the sheep."

Leader: Surely goodness and love will follow me all the days of my life,

People: And I will dwell in the house of the Lord forever.

John 10:7-15; Psalm 23

Waiting and Trusting

Leader: Find rest, O my soul, in God alone.

People: My hope comes from him.

Narr. 1: Then the word of the Lord came to Jonah a second time: "Go to the great city of Nineveh and proclaim to it the message I give you."

Narr. 2: Jonah obeyed the word of the Lord and went to Nineveh.

Leader: He alone is my rock and my salvation.

People: He is my fortress, I will not be shaken.

Narr. 1: Now Nineveh was a very important city—a visit required three days.

Narr. 2: On the first day, Jonah started into the city.

Narr. 1: He proclaimed: "Forty more days and Nineveh will be overturned."

Narr. 2: The Ninevites believed God.

Leader: My salvation and my honor depend on God.

People: He is my mighty rock, my refuge.

Narr. 1: They declared a fast, and all of them, from the greatest to the least, put on sackcloth.

Narr. 2: When God saw what they did and how they turned from their evil ways, he had compassion and did not bring upon them the destruction he had threatened.

Leader: Trust in him at all times, O people. Pour out your hearts to him.

People: God is our refuge.

Leader: Lowborn men are but a breath, the highborn are but a lie. If weighed on a balance, they are nothing; together they are only a breath.

MEN: You, O God, are strong.

WOMEN: You, O Lord, are loving.

LEADER: Do not trust in extortion or take pride in stolen goods. Though your riches increase, do not set your heart on them.

MEN: You, O God, are strong.

WOMEN: You, O Lord, are loving.

LEADER: One thing God has spoken, two things have I heard: You, O God, are strong. You, O Lord, are loving.

PEOPLE: God is our refuge.

PSALM 62:5-12; JONAH 3:1-5, 10

In the Potter's Hand

SOLO 1: This is the word that came to Jeremiah from the Lord: "Go down to the potter's house, and there I will give you my message."

SOLO 2: So I went down to the potter's house, and I saw him working at the wheel.

SOLO 1: But the pot he was shaping from the clay was marred in his hands;

SOLO 2: So the potter formed it into another pot, shaping it as seemed best to him.

SOLO 1: Then the word of the Lord came to me: "O house of Israel, can I not do with you as this potter does?" declares the Lord.

SOLO 2: Like clay in the hand of the potter, so are you in my hand, O house of Israel.

SOLO 1: Then why does God still blame us?

PEOPLE: For who can resist his will?

LEADER: But who are you, O man, to talk back to God?

PEOPLE: O Lord, we are the clay and you are the potter.

LEADER: Does the clay say to the potter, "What are you making?"

PEOPLE: Does your work say, "He has no hands"?

LEADER: Does not the potter have the right to make out of the same lump of clay some pottery for noble purposes and some for common use?

PEOPLE: O Lord, you are our Father.

LEADER: We are the clay, you are the potter.

PEOPLE: O Lord, we are all the work of your hand.

JEREMIAH 18:1-6; ROMANS 9:19-21; ISAIAH 64:8; 45:9

To All Who Thirst

Leader: Come, all you who are thirsty.

Choir: Come to me, all you who are weary and burdened.

People: Come to the waters. Come to me.

Men: You who have no money, come.

Women: Come, buy and eat.

Leader: Come, buy wine and milk.

Choir: Come, buy without money and without cost.

People: The poor and needy search for water,

Women: But there is none;

Leader: I will pour water on the thirsty land,

Choir: And streams on the dry ground;

Leader: I will pour out my Spirit on your offspring,

People: And my blessing on your descendants.

Solo: The invitation comes from the Source of all satisfaction: to the weary and worn He says, "Come and find rest." To the parched and thirsty he holds out the promise of refreshment. It was Jesus who offered the quenching water of life to a Samaritan woman.

Leader: Jesus came to a town in Samaria called Sychar. Jacob's well was there, and Jesus, tired from the journey, sat down by the well.

Women: When a Samaritan woman came to draw water,

Men: Jesus said to her, "Will you give me a drink?"

Woman: The Samaritan woman said to him, "You are a Jew and I am a Samaritan woman. How can you ask me for a drink?"

Men: Jesus answered her, "If you knew the gift of God and who it is that asks you for a drink, you would have asked him and he would have given you living water."

Woman: "Sir," the woman said, "where can you get this living water?"

Men: Jesus said, "Everyone who drinks this water will be thirsty again, but whoever drinks the water I give him will never thirst."

Leader: And then Jesus added,

Men: Indeed, the water I give him will become in him a spring of water welling up to eternal life.

Woman: The woman said to Jesus, "Sir, give me this water so that I won't get thirsty again."

Leader: Jesus stood and said in a loud voice,

Choir: If anyone is thirsty, let him come to me and drink.

People: Whoever believes in me, streams of living water will flow from within him.

Leader: Come, all you who are thirsty.

People: Come to me, all you who are weary and burdened.

Choir: Come!

All: Come to me.

Isaiah 55:1; Matthew 11:28; Isaiah 41:17; 44:3; John 4:5-15; 7:37-38

In Christ

Leader: If you have any encouragement from being united in Christ . . .

People: We have his encouragement!

Leader: If you have any comfort from his love . . .

People: We are comforted in his love!

Leader: If you have any fellowship with the Spirit . . .

People: We have fellowship with the Spirit!

Leader: If you have any tenderness and compassion . . .

People: We are tenderly compassionate!

Leader: Then be one in spirit and purpose.

All: In Christ we will be like-minded and love.

Philippians 2:1-2

Scripture Index

Old Testament

Genesis
1:26-27, 31 ... 70
1:27 ... 75
1:27-28, 31 ... 51
2:15-17, 25 ... 51
2:23-24 ... 75
3:1-8, 16-19 ... 51
4:2-8 ... 16
5:21-24 ... 16
6:17-19, 22 ... 16
7:1, 12 ... 16
8:6, 15, 20-22 ... 16
9:1 ... 17
22:1-19 ... 11

Exodus
14:29-31 ... 89
15:1-7, 11, 13, 17-18 ... 89

Deuteronomy
8:6-13, 18 ... 90

1 Samuel
16:1-13 ... 12

2 Kings
5:1 ... 24

Job
7:1-7 ... 87

Psalms
1 ... 66
7:1-11, 17 ... 91
19:7-11 ... 55
22 ... 34
23 ... 95, 96
24 ... 81
24:3-4 ... 58
24:3-4, 7-10 ... 55
27:1, 13-14 ... 12
31:9-13 ... 33
36:7-9 ... 61
37:11 ... 58
62:5-12 ... 97
65 ... 82
70:1-4 ... 32
72:1-8 ... 47
72:1-14 ... 22
78:1-4 ... 77
84:11 ... 95
89:8-13 ... 95
92:1-2, 4 ... 64
93:1 ... 95
96 ... 20
116:1-9, 12-14, 17-19 ... 83
118:19-29 ... 84
119:9-12, 105 ... 64
126:1-6 ... 85
133 ... 36
147:1-11 ... 87

Ecclesiastes
3:1-2 ... 63

Song of Songs
2:15 ... 75
8:6-7 ... 75, 76

Isaiah
2:3-5 ... 47
2:5 ... 55
7:14 ... 19
9:2, 6-7 ... 20, 53
9:6 ... 69
11:1-10 ... 47
12:2-6 ... 55
35:1-6 ... 85
41:17 ... 99
42:6-7 ... 61
44:3 ... 99
45:9 ... 98
49:6-7 ... 61
50:4-9 ... 32
52:13—53:12 ... 49
53:6 ... 51
55:1 ... 58, 99
55:10-13 ... 64
58:3-9 ... 65
60:1-6 ... 22
64:8 ... 98

Jeremiah
17:5-8 ... 66
18:1-6 ... 98
33:15-16 ... 55

Ezekiel
37:1-14 ... 28

Daniel
3 ... 13
9:16, 18-19 ... 68

Hosea
4:1 68
4:1-3 67
6:1-6 67
10:12 67

Joel
2:12-13 65

Amos
5:11-12, 14-15, 24 68

Jonah
3:1-5, 10 97

Micah
5:2, 4-5 19

Zephaniah
3:16-17 85

Malachi
4:1-2 63

New Testament

Matthew
2:1-11 22
5:1-10 58
11:28 99
13:3-8 63
19:6 75
21:1-11 84
24:36-42 73
25:34 58
27:11-25 33
28:18-20 63

Luke
1:26-38 19
1:46-53 47
2:1-19 20
4:16, 18-19, 21 24
4:21-30 24
6:20-26 66
7:9 16
24:13-34 37
24:49 39

John
1:1-14 53
1:9 25
3:1-17 57
3:3, 16 63
4:5-15 99
4:35-38 72
7:37-38 99
9:1-39 25
9:4 72
10:7-15 96
11:1-45 28
12:20-36 61
13:1-15 30
13:18-30 32
14:15-18 39
19:17-30 34
20:19-29 36

Acts
2:1-4, 17-18, 21 39
4:32-33 36
6 42
7 42
8 42
8:26-39 43
9 42

Romans
3:23 51
8:36-37 63
9:19-21 98
11:33-36 88
12:20-21 24
13:11-12 73

1 Corinthians
1:7-9 73
1:18-31 59
2:9-10 88
11:23-26 30
13 76
13:4-8 75

2 Corinthians
6:2 63

Galatians
5:22-23 70
6:9 72

Ephesians
3:2-12 77
5:8-14 25
6:10-12 58

Philippians
1:1-4, 6, 9-11, 18-19, 21 69
2:1-2 100
2:5-11 69
4:3-7, 9 71

Colossians
1:1-6, 13-16, 18-23 52
3:1-11 71

1 Thessalonians
4:14, 16-17 92
5:23-24 74

2 Timothy
2:8, 11-13 92

Philemon
4-6 86

Hebrews
1:1-2 53
4:14 16
10:5-10 55
11 16

James
2:13 58
3:18 58
5:7-9 74

1 Peter
3:14-15 58

2 Peter
3:8-14 74

1 John
1:5-7 60
3:1, 11, 18 76

Revelation
1:1, 3-4, 8 93
2:7 93
7:17 58
21:1-14, 18-27 93
22:21 93

Seasonal and Topical Index

Advent 19, 47, 52, 53, 61
Assurance 71, 87, 95, 96, 97, 98
Belief/Faith 11, 13, 16, 25, 36, 37
Christian Fellowship 60
Christlikeness 58, 69, 71, 86, 92
Christmas 20, 22, 53
Christ the King 52, 61
Communion 30
Easter 36, 37
Epiphany 22
Evangelism 43, 49, 63, 99
Faith/Belief 11, 13, 16, 25, 36, 37
Family 75, 77
God's Attributes 95, 96, 97
God's Provisions 11, 12, 19, 47, 49, 58, 59, 61, 90, 95, 99
God's Word 64
Good Friday 34
Heaven 93
Holy Week 30, 32, 33, 34, 84
Justice 91
Labor Day 72
Lent 31, 49, 59, 65
Marriage 75, 76
Mercy 47
Mission 24, 43
New Birth 57
New Year 63, 98
Obedience 19, 55, 60, 66, 71
Palm Sunday 84
Passion Sunday 34
Pentecost 39
Praise 64, 82, 83, 84, 85, 88, 89, 91
Repentance 49, 51, 67
Revival 28, 57, 65, 67
Salvation 55, 57, 61, 63
Second Advent 73, 74, 92
Social Concern 24, 61, 65, 68
Stewardship 81, 82
Thanksgiving 81, 82, 83
Unity 77, 100
Witness 13, 40, 43